GREAT MILITARY LEADERS
of the 20TH Century

Douglas MacArthur
Mao Zedong
George S. Patton
John J. Pershing
Erwin J.E. Rommel
H. Norman Schwarzkopf

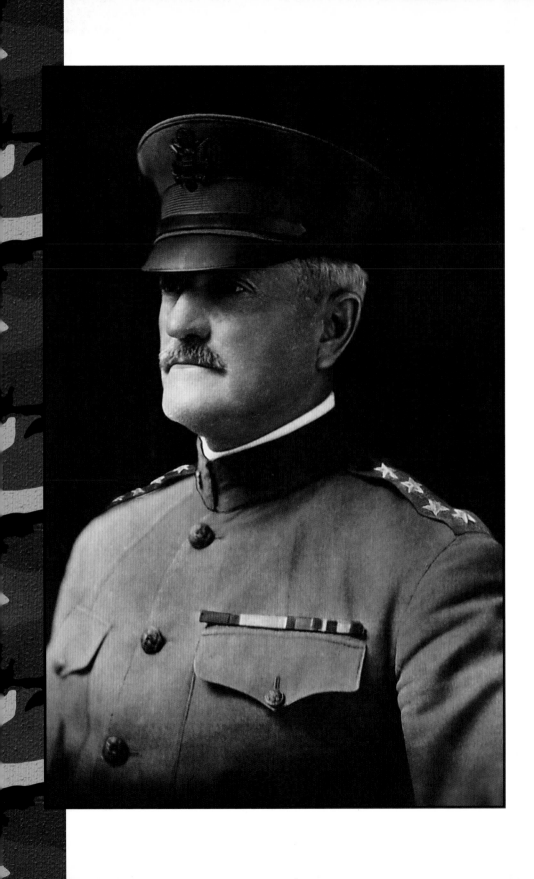

GREAT MILITARY LEADERS
of the 20TH Century

JOHN J. PERSHING

TIM McNEESE

INTRODUCTION BY
CASPAR W. WEINBERGER

SERIES CONSULTING EDITOR
EARLE RICE JR.

CHELSEA HOUSE
PUBLISHERS
A Haights Cross Communications Company
Philadelphia

FRONTIS: **Hand-tinted portrait of Pershing.**

CHELSEA HOUSE PUBLISHERS

VP, NEW PRODUCT DEVELOPMENT Sally Cheney
DIRECTOR OF PRODUCTION Kim Shinners
CREATIVE MANAGER Takeshi Takahashi
MANUFACTURING MANAGER Diann Grasse

STAFF FOR **JOHN J. PERSHING**

EXECUTIVE EDITOR Lee Marcott
PRODUCTION ASSISTANT Megan Emery
PICTURE RESEARCHER Noelle Nardone
SERIES & COVER DESIGNER Keith Trego
LAYOUT 21st Century Publishing and Communications, Inc.

A Haights Cross Communications ✦ Company

http://www.chelseahouse.com

First Printing

1 3 5 7 9 8 6 4 2

Library of Congress Cataloging-in-Publication Data

McNeese, Tim.
    John J. Pershing / by Tim McNeese.
        p. cm. -- (Great military leaders of the 20th century) Includes
index.
Summary: Reviews the life and battles of General "Black Jack"
Pershing, who had more than thirty years of field experience when he
was tapped to lead the American Expeditionary Forces during World
War I.
    ISBN 0-7910-7404-8
  1. Pershing, John J. (John Joseph), 1860-1948--Juvenile literature. 2.
Generals--United States--Biography--Juvenile literature. 3. United
States. Army--Biography--Juvenile literature. 4. United States--
History, Military--20th century. [1. Pershing, John J. (John Joseph),
1860-1948. 2. Generals. 3. United States--History, Military--20th century.] I. Title. II. Series.
E181.P486 2003
355.3'32'092

2003008914

TABLE OF CONTENTS

INTRODUCTION

by Caspar W. Weinberger

At a time when it is ever more apparent that the world will need skilled and bold military leaders, it is both appropriate and necessary that school history courses include studies of great military leaders.

Democracies, for the most part, are basically not greatly interested in military leadership or military matters in general. Fortunately, in the United States we have sufficient interest and volunteers for military service so that we can maintain and staff a very strong military with volunteers—people who want to serve.

That is very fortunate indeed for us. Volunteers and those who decide of their own free will that they want to be in the military are, generally speaking, easier to train, and to retain in the services, and their morale is markedly higher than that of conscripts. Furthermore, the total effect of a draft, based on our Vietnam experience, can be very bad—indeed it can polarize the country as a whole.

One of the best ways of ensuring that we will continue to have enough volunteers in the future is to study the great accomplishments of our past military leaders—the small group of leaders and others who contributed so much to our past greatness and our present strength.

Not all of these leaders have been Americans, but the

example that all of them set are well worth studying in our schools. Of the six military leaders chosen by Chelsea House's "Great Military Leaders of the 20th Century," I had the privilege of serving under and with two.

In World War II, after two years of volunteer service in the infantry at home and in the Pacific, I was transferred from the 41st Infantry Division then in New Guinea, to General Douglas MacArthur's intelligence staff in Manila, in the Philippines. One of my assignments was to prepare drafts of the general's daily communiqué to other theatre commanders around the world. This required seeing all of the major military cable and intelligence information, and digesting the most important items for his daily report to the other war theatres of the world. It also required a familiarity with our plans to carry the war to the enemy as soon as sufficient strength had been transferred to our theatre from Europe.

The invasion of Japan toward which all the planning was aiming would have been a very difficult and costly operation. Most of the tentative plans called for landing our force on one of the southern Japanese islands, and another force on Honshu, north of Tokyo.

We know that Japan's troops would have fought fiercely and very skillfully once their homeland was invaded. In fact, all of our plans forecast that we would lose virtually all of the first two U.S. divisions that landed. That was one of the main reasons that President Harry Truman concluded we had to use the atomic bomb. That ended the war, and all landings taken in Japan were peaceful and unopposed.

Many years later, when I was secretary of defense under President Ronald Reagan, a part of my duties was to recommend generals and admirals for various U.S. and NATO regional commands. Fulfilling this duty led me to interview several possible candidates for the post of commander in chief of our Central Command, which had jurisdiction over our many military activities in the Middle East.

My strong recommendation, accepted by the president, was that he name General H. Norman Schwarzkopf to lead the Central Command. A short time later, General Schwarzkopf led our forces in that region to the great military victory of the Gulf War.

General MacArthur and General Schwarzkopf shared many of the same qualities. Both were very experienced army officers tested by many widely different conditions all over the world. Both were calm, resolute, and inspirational leaders. Both were superb military planners and developers of complex and very large-scale military operations. Both achieved great military successes; both had the best interest of all our troops at heart; and both were leaders in the best sense of the word. They both had the ability and skills necessary to work with military and civilian leaders of our allies and friends in all parts of the globe.

It is vitally important for our future as a democracy, a superpower and a country whose strengths have helped save freedom and peace, that our children and our schools know far more about these leaders and countless others like them who serve the cause of peace with freedom so well and so faithfully. Their lives and the lives of others like them will be a great inspiration for us and for later generations who need to know what America at its best can accomplish.

The other military leaders whose lives are presented in this series include a German, General Erwin Rommel, and the former Communist China leader, Mao Zedong.

General Rommel won many preliminary battles in the desert war of World War II before losing the decisive battle of El Alamein. He had to develop and execute his tactics for desert fighting under conditions not previously experienced by him or his troops. He also became one of the masters of the art of tank warfare.

Mao Zedong had to train, develop, arm, and deploy huge numbers of Chinese soldiers to defeat the organized and experienced forces of Chiang Kai-shek's Nationalist government. He accomplished this and, in comparatively short time, won the military victories that transformed his country.

Both of these generals had to learn, very quickly, the new tactics needed to cope with rapidly changing conditions. In short, they had to be flexible, inventive, and willing and able to fight against larger opposing forces and in unfamiliar environments.

This whole series demonstrates that great military success requires many of the qualities and skills required for success in other fields of endeavor. Military history is indeed a vital part of the whole story of mankind, and one of the best ways of studying that history is to study the lives of those who succeeded by their leadership in this vital field.

CASPAR W. WEINBERGER
CHAIRMAN, *FORBES* INC
MARCH 2003

CASPAR W. WEINBERGER was the fifteenth U.S. secretary of defense, serving under President Ronald Reagan from 1981 to 1987, longer than any previous defense secretary except Robert McNamara (served 1961–1968). Weinberger is also an author who has written books about his experiences in the Reagan administration and about U.S. military capabilities.

1

"Cool as a Bowl of Cracked Ice"

The morning dawned clear and balmy in Cuba. First Lieutenant John J. Pershing scanned the landscape in front of him as several American units prepared to make an assault against a well-entrenched Spanish force, hidden in the dense undergrowth of a lush tropical forest. Scanning enemy territory, Pershing could see nearly invisible lines of entrenchment situated half a mile away on the opposite side of the Aguadores River. Dotted by blockhouses protecting the crest of the hills of San Juan, the entrenchment cut across his army's approach.

Pershing spotted movement along the left side of the first hill. There, a solitary Spanish sentinel stood holding the reins of his horse. To the west, Pershing could see the outer defenses

Pershing got his first taste of battle while he was a lieutenant serving in the Spanish-American War. Leading the 10th cavalry through the thick Cuban jungle and facing deadly enemy fire, Pershing retained his composure and earned a reputation for leadership.

of Santiago. Farther away, Pershing could make out the church spires, stone buildings, and towers of the city. The Cuban outpost looked like a ghost town, the civilian population having evacuated when the Americans approached. As Pershing continued to scan the landscape, he could see in the foothills to the northeast, commanding a rocky outcropping, the stone fortress and ring of smaller blockhouses of El Caney. It was here that the Spanish had taken up defensive positions. Pershing knew what every other American officer and enlisted man preparing for the assault understood: These blockhouses would have to be captured—and the Spanish would not make that goal an easy one for the newly arrived U.S. forces to accomplish.

At 6:30 A.M., the quiet of the post-dawn jungle was suddenly shattered by rifle fire as American infantry under the command of Brigadier General H. W. Lawton began an advance. From his field position, Pershing tried intently to see exactly where the enemy was located. He and other cavalrymen had orders to remain in position and postpone their advance until Lawton's men had routed the Spanish. This command led to an anxious delay for Pershing and his comrades. Lawton had hoped his assault would be completed within a couple of hours. He met with stiff resistance, however, and his right flank began to crumble. By 8:20 A.M., Brigadier William Rufus Shafter had waited as long as he could, and he ordered his artillery battery to fire on San Juan Hill. The barrage turned out to be pointless, since Shafter's guns were too far away to hit Spanish positions, and the smoke they left in the air gave away the American positions. Spanish guns opened fire on the Americans below the hills, causing significant casualties. Some of the American artillery actually hit some cavalry troopers who were positioned ahead of the U.S. cannon positions. Near Pershing, American guns hit a sugar mill.

At 9:00 A.M., the cavalry began to move, including Pershing, who mounted his horse and prepared to take part in the first major battle of his military career. Even as his men moved forward, though, the Americans were bunching up on a narrow road, unable to make significant progress. Included in the confusion were the men of Pershing's 10th cavalry, "its men piling ahead toward the river, packing beyond the road into the bush, jamming into a solid, unsortable mass."[1] In the midst of the fight, a great yellow U.S. army balloon was launched to provide a way to spot the enemy. The balloon, however, merely drew Spanish fire and showed the enemy exactly where the Americans were situated in the thick jungle.

Along a riverbank, Pershing crouched down as chaos hampered the American assault up San Juan Heights. He later wrote, "Remaining there under this galling fire of exploding shrapnel and deadly mauser [*sic*] volleys the minutes seemed like hours."[2] He received orders to take his men across the Aguadores, where they would be less vulnerable to enemy fire.

Without accurate maps of the Cuban jungle before them, General Joseph Wheeler's cavalry units made slow, awkward progress. As the volunteer unit known as the Rough Riders, led by former Assistant Secretary of the Navy Theodore Roosevelt, and the 10th cavalry, consisting largely of African-American troops, moved along a narrow trail, they met Spanish gunfire. Pershing referred to the opening shots as a "veritable hail of shot and shell."[3] Still, even as a recent graduate of West Point took a hit and fell dead nearby, Pershing showed no fear.

The American forces pushed forward under fire from the Spanish guns spread across the hilly Cuban landscape. Complicating matters for the Americans was the fact that their older, black-powder Springfield rifles sent out thick clouds of smoke when fired, which helped the Spanish to locate the American troops easily. The Spanish, on the other hand, were using newer Mausers, which had a greater range and used smokeless powder.

The thick undergrowth of jungle caused American units to bunch up, slowing their movement even further. With bayonets, they hacked at the "thorned vegetation, high grasses, and thickets, with bullets from the Spaniards' Mauser rifles continually hitting home."[4] Although these troops were cavalry, only a handful of officers had horses. Nearly everyone advanced on foot, which was fortunate for many, since they were better targets for the Spanish hiding in the hills above when they were mounted. Half of the 10th cavalry's 22 white officers were picked off in short order.

During the Spanish-American War, the African-American soldiers of Lieutenant Pershing's 10th cavalry showed immense courage in the taking of Kettle Hill. Despite well-entrenched opposition, Pershing's men were able to reach their objective.

In the action, Pershing later remembered seeing the aged veteran Joe Wheeler, who had seen action as a Confederate cavalry officer during the Civil War, on his horse in the middle of a jungle stream. As Pershing approached Wheeler, an enemy artillery shot hit the water between them, sending up a dousing spray that drenched both men.

Pershing finally succeeded in getting his men across the river. They were then in position to attack Kettle Hill, one of the two primary objectives of the assault, but they waited for orders to advance. Spanish sniper fire continued to add to their casualties. For 30 minutes, Pershing's African-American troops remained hunkered down in the lush Cuban vegetation, seeking vainly to spot the enemy above.

By noon, Lawton's forces had reached El Caney. Casualties had been high, and the general assault that was to follow in Lawton's wake was still unorganized. Portions of regiments had become separated from one another. Entire brigades had not yet been deployed forward. Shafter, who was overweight and ill with a fever, began to doubt the possibility of success in this heated jungle fight. Though the American commander did not know it at the time, the Spanish force holding them back numbered only 600.

Through the shots firing all around, Pershing spotted his captain, George Ayres. Ayres yelled to his first lieutenant to show him the way up the hill. Pershing pointed out the way. Ayres later recalled how "the gallant Pershing . . . was as cool as a bowl of cracked ice."[5] The composed lieutenant then turned to search for a second squadron he had lost in the confusion, one directly under the command of Major T. J. Wint, who, like Ayres, asked Pershing for directions. Historian Frank Vandiver describes what happened next:

> Saluting, [Pershing] offered guidance. Wint . . . asked Jack [Pershing] to lead on. Quickly Wint must have wondered about his judgment. Pershing took the column squarely into an impenetrable thicket, where he told the troopers to knock down wire entanglements and press on toward the river's edge. Fire picked up, and the jungle shivered with alien bullets, but Pershing led the way. As the men reached a semblance of clearing they saw the river, and beyond it they glimpsed Kettle Hill. Its jaunty red-roofed building on top became every man's objective.[6]

Even as the troops spotted their destination, no direct frontal assault was ordered immediately. The blue-clad American troops remained pinned down by deadly accurate enemy fire. The battle had reached the point of no return. Shafter would either have to order a retreat or the Americans would have to take action and move forward into the face of the enemy's positions on the high ground. At 1:30 P.M., the decision was made. Orders from headquarters arrived, instructing all units to advance. The charge had already begun, however. Officers who were angry about their inaction had begun to make their own charges earlier, with their men following closely behind. Pershing sent his men forward, too, up the southern rise of Kettle Hill. He later described the scene:

> In the underbrush and tall grass it was difficult to keep alignments and the troops soon became very much mixed. But each officer or soldier next in rank took charge of the line or group immediately in his vicinity, halting to fire at each good opportunity. The men took cover only when ordered to do so and exposed themselves fearlessly in crossing the open spaces.[7]

Soon, the African-American troopers of the 10th cavalry were moving with the Rough Riders up the hill, despite heavy fire from Spanish rifles. The hill itself provided little cover for the advancing Americans, but they continued up each sloping foot of exposed terrain, intent on their goal. As American units rushed up Kettle Hill, Roosevelt's Rough Riders swung to the left, up neighboring San Juan Hill. Suddenly, Spanish resistance tapered, then fell silent as the enemy surrendered its positions atop Kettle Hill. Climbing and firing up the hill, Pershing reached the top to find the enemy entrenchments abandoned. The battle was not over, though. Pershing's new objective was San Juan Hill, to the left. Having run the enemy off one hill, all units continued their advance toward the next hill. The fight had not yet been won, but John J. Pershing had experienced his first taste of real battle.

Missouri Born
and Raised

One of America's greatest generals was born just as the United States was preparing to go to war with itself. John Joseph Pershing was born on September 13, 1860, in a modest farmhouse near the small town of Laclede in north-central Missouri. John Joseph was the first of the Pershings' nine children. He had bright blue eyes and hair so blond it was nearly white. Townspeople called him "Johnny." Within his family, he was often called "Jack."

This new arrival was the first of five generations of Pershings who had first come to America from Europe in 1749. That year, Frederick Pfoershing had left the German region of Alsace behind, bound for America. With no money, Frederick

John Joseph Pershing was born on the eve of the Civil War in this modest farmhouse near Laclede, Missouri. Since many Missourians supported the Confederacy, Pershing's father's decision to support the Union cause was not always popular with his neighbors.

worked as an indentured servant for nearly two years, during which time he married Maria Elizabeth in York, Pennsylvania. While living as pioneers in a log cabin named "Coventry," Frederick shortened his last name to an Americanized "Pershing." This first generation of

American Pershings produced six children, including Daniel, the youngest.

When Frederick died in 1794, Daniel set out on his own, marrying in 1798. Daniel Pershing was a coal miner who later became a circuit-riding Methodist preacher. He and his wife had a child, Joseph Mercer Pershing, in 1810, who grew up to run his father's farm. Joseph married and on March 1, 1834, his wife gave birth to John Joseph Pershing's father, John Fletcher Pershing.

The new parents, John Fletcher Pershing and Anne Elizabeth Thompson, had not been in Missouri long, having arrived in 1858, before their first child was born. John Fletcher had taken a job as a section foreman on the Hannibal and St. Joseph Railroad. The elder Pershing was an ambitious and energetic man, and he soon found himself operating a general store and serving as Laclede's postmaster. General John Pershing remembered his father as a strict disciplinarian, but a wonderful family man who was devoted to the proper upbringing of his children.

As the Pershings worked to establish themselves during their early days in Laclede, the rumbling threat of a war that would divide the country's North and South appeared imminent during the months after John Joseph Pershing's birth. As slaveholding states broke away from the North in 1860 and 1861, the future of one slave state, Missouri, remained undecided. Missourians began to take sides, some supporting the states' rights, proslavery position of the South and others remaining loyal to the Union. The Pershing household was determined to support the Union, even though many of Anne Elizabeth's family eventually fought for the Confederacy.

The Pershings' position was not popular with all their neighbors. When Mrs. Pershing sewed an American flag that John Fletcher placed outside their house, some supporters of the South threatened to come to the Pershing home and tear the banner down. Pershing informed them that if anyone attempted to do so, "they should carry with them a long pine box [for a coffin]," [8] because he intended to shoot anyone who touched his flag. The threats suddenly stopped.

Once the war began in April 1861, John Fletcher Pershing, already a storekeeper, began to provide food and other supplies to Union soldiers. He sold items that the army did not give the troops, including tobacco, cookies, cakes, fruits, knives, wooden combs, medicines, and even joke books.

The war went on for four years. The violence reached the town of Laclede itself when, on June 18, 1864, a band of pro-Confederates, fighters who had not officially joined the Southern army, rode into town and began to threaten local Union supporters. Two Laclede citizens were gunned down, one of them while trying to run for safety. The raiders were especially interested in destroying Pershing's store, since it supplied Northern troops. When they burst into the store, however, Pershing fled out the back door to his nearby house, only to return with a double-barreled shotgun. General John Joseph Pershing later remembered how he and his two-year-old brother, James, "huddled on the floor until the raiders departed." [9] Before the irregulars left Laclede, they ransacked the town, including Pershing's store.

Later, a detachment of Union troops was assigned to the small Missouri community. Young John Pershing was captivated by the blue-clad Union men. His mother sewed a small blue uniform for her son, so he could dress like his military heroes. The Union troops he visited were delighted with the four-year-old's interest in them. "I certainly saw a lot of soldiers as a child," Pershing remembered, "and liked to be with them." [10]

The war finally ended in the spring of 1865, and Laclede once again became a bustling, growing northern Missouri town, although it still had rough elements. After the war, John Fletcher Pershing remained dedicated to the strict upbringing of his children. Of the Pershing offspring, six survived their younger years, including three boys and three girls. The children had regular chores, since their father believed in hard work. As John Joseph grew older, his chores changed from plucking weeds to planting a garden to working in the family stable.

When school was not in session, young John played with his male friends, running around town and acting out battles on the old defensive mounds that had been erected during the Civil War. He and his comrades stole peaches from a neighbor's orchard, camped out together, held wrestling matches, and swam in the local watering hole. As Laclede grew into a prosperous Midwestern community, John Joseph Pershing grew up, too.

These were halcyon days for John Joseph. His family was well-off and the economy was booming. His father was a leading citizen in their town, and his mother was always there to support her children and their education. She also drilled them on lessons of faith and morality:

> Mother knew her Bible, believed in it, and expected her family to believe. Johnny accepted the form but worried little about the faith. And yet there was one essential about life that his mother taught him, one that would linger with him always: "There were moral obligations that it was the duty of everyone to fulfill."[11]

Despite boyish lapses, it was a lesson that John Joseph Pershing took seriously for the rest of his life.

As Pershing approached his teenage years, he formed a keen interest in firearms, as did his friends. Together, they tromped across the Missouri countryside, hunting everything from geese and quail to rabbits and raccoons. Once, when John discovered some old army pistols around the house, he took one and cleaned and oiled it until it looked usable. When he loaded it, he accidentally fired it, the lead ball burying itself in the railing of a mahogany bed. After that bit of foolishness, Pershing remembered, "I was forbidden to play with loaded revolvers."[12]

John's preteen years saw a dramatic downturn in the fortunes of the Pershing family. In 1873, just as John Joseph turned 13, the United States fell into an economic depression. Land prices dropped, and John Fletcher Pershing was forced to sell property he had owned for several years to pay the mortgages on newly acquired property. Slowly, the poor economy ate away almost all the family assets. For a time, John Joseph worked the family farm for his father. Then, an 1875 drought and a plague of grasshoppers killed the corn crop. The general store had to be sold, and eventually, the family farm went on the auction block, too.

With the loss of the farm, John Joseph Pershing had few options left. In 1876, at age 16, he had completed his public school studies. By 1878, he decided to take the examination for his teaching certification, which he passed. The only opening he could find, however, was as a teacher at the Laclede Negro School.

Taking a teaching position at the all-black school caused some problems for John Joseph. African-American parents refused to send their children to the school until a black teacher was hired. When they finally gave in, local whites criticized Pershing for teaching blacks. Even inside the schoolhouse, the new teacher faced problems. He was only 18 years old and some of his students were older and bigger than he was. Pershing dealt with issues as they came, running his classroom with strict discipline.

After a few months, he took a teaching position at Prairie Mound, a small town ten miles (16 kilometers) from Laclede. There, he had to deal with a new set of bullies, but he managed to bring his 45 students, who ranged in age from six to 21, under control. Although he did not remain a teacher for long, he later wrote, "My experience in teaching was most valuable and there is no doubt that I learned more than any of my pupils." He added, "Especially in the practical lessons of managing others." [13]

For years, Pershing had dreamed of becoming a lawyer. If he could enroll in the First District Normal School in Kirksville (present-day Truman State University), just 60 miles (97 kilometers) from Laclede, and graduate, he could teach in better schools and eventually attend the University of Missouri at Columbia to fulfill his ambition to practice law. He decided that his savings would pay for his first three months of school.

Arriving by train in Kirksville, a thriving northern Missouri community of 3,000 people, in the spring of 1880, Pershing settled in, determined to achieve good grades. His rigorous studies included courses in literature, physical geography, algebra, geometry, Latin, history, zoology, physics, and the art of teaching. Pershing learned a lot from the faculty at Kirksville. There were about ten professors, qualified teachers who took a serious approach to higher learning. The academics were solid, and the school expected discipline from its students. Classes began right on schedule—in fact, the school was the first in the country to have a clock-bell system.

After the spring semester, Pershing returned to Prairie Mound much more confident in his skills as a teacher. He was now 20 years old, had matured in his build and face, and looked more like a serious scholar:

> A certainty was in him now, the arrogance of confidence. He might have been Foppish—he had learned to like good clothes and wore them well—but somehow remained wholly manly. His students liked him and learned from him, his family loved him, and girls enjoyed his company.[14]

After the end of his teaching term, Pershing returned to Kirksville for more study. His sister Elizabeth went with him to enroll in Kirksville, too. The two siblings enjoyed one another's company. They spent time together and helped each other with their schoolwork.

Then, in September 1881, while sitting in his sister's room, Pershing was reading a newspaper from home. He saw an announcement that caught his eye: "Notice is hereby given that there will be a competitive examination held at Trenton, Missouri . . . for the purpose of selecting one Cadet for the Military Academy at West Point." In fact, Pershing knew little about West Point, only that great Civil War generals—such as Robert E. Lee, Ulysses S. Grant, William T. Sherman, and Thomas "Stonewall" Jackson—had been educated there. He knew one other thing as well: An appointment to West Point would give him a chance to go on to higher education. After Elizabeth encouraged him to try for the West Point appointment, Pershing decided to give it his best effort.

After taking a leave from Kirksville, Pershing researched the subjects with which he needed to become more familiar. Elizabeth helped her brother study for the difficult examination. They studied together "over a lamp-lit table, sister asking endless questions, brother struggling for the answers."[15] When the time arrived,

At the age of 21, Pershing made a decision that changed his life. Seeing his chance to pursue an education, he entered a contest whose winner would be selected as a cadet for the U.S. Military Academy at West Point (seen here). When the contest was over, Pershing was the last man standing.

Pershing went to Trenton, where he was one of 18 young men taking the exam.

Most of the exam consisted of written questions, but each boy fielded some portions one question at a time, with those who failed to answer questions correctly dropping out. Finally, only two boys were left standing, and Pershing was one of them. The last question was about grammar, and Pershing replied correctly after the other young man missed the answer. John Joseph Pershing, age

21, was on his way to West Point, located 1,000 miles (1,609 kilometers) back east in New York State. Before now, he had never even left the state of Missouri.

Despite having passed the entrance exam at Trenton, Pershing still had to take yet another examination before he would be officially accepted into West Point. Pershing heard about a preparatory school near the West Point grounds that was open to would-be appointees, where they could study for the final examination. John Joseph returned to Kirksville, gave the administration the news that he was leaving for West Point, then went home to Laclede, where he informed his surprised parents of his success. His mother seemed skeptical. "But John, you are not going into the army, are you?" she asked with concern.[16] Despite her reservations, Anna Elizabeth Pershing supported her son's decision and helped him get to New York, where he arrived in January 1882.

Pershing later wrote about how he crammed for the final examination, studying "page after page of stuff that we forgot completely before plebe [freshman] camp was over."[17] In the summer of 1882, Pershing passed the exam and soon found himself entering the hallowed halls of the U.S. Military Academy at West Point. The next four years were filled with more trials and challenges than John Joseph Pershing could ever have imagined. Pershing and his fellow first-year recruits numbered 129 when their course of study began. Four years later, only 77 remained.

As that first school year—1882—opened, West Point's superintendent was Oliver Otis Howard, a one-armed veteran of the Civil War, but he was soon succeeded by another Civil War hero, Wesley Merritt. Merritt ran the academy strictly. Drilling, marching, and studying made students face a constant barrage of activity and stress. The courses ranged from mathematics to history to

French to military arts, such as fencing, musketry, gunnery, and horsemanship. Of all his subjects, Pershing had the most trouble with French. His military skills were another matter. Pershing proved to be the best marksman in his class.

Almost all plebes sometimes received demerits for infractions, or violations, of the academy's rules. In four years, Pershing received 200 demerits—equal to nearly one a week. These negative marks did not take away the positive qualities for which he became recognized during his training at West Point, though:

> [A]s an immaculate and snappy and severe and disciplined soldier of perfect military bearing, he was unsurpassable. He had the sharp-speaking, dominating, exacting qualities that made for a drillmaster, the command personality. The military ideal of complete precision married to the concept that if a job is worth doing it is worth doing well seized him.[18]

These traits won Pershing the attention of others, and he was elected class president.

He continued his second-year studies still intent on conquering the "rigors of the institution by his own efforts. He never relied on anything else."[19] At the end of his second year, Pershing and his fellow cadets received their first leave, having never left the West Point grounds during the first two terms. Pershing went home to Laclede to visit his family.

After he completed his third year at West Point, Pershing received his greatest honor yet—he was selected as first captain of the Corps of Cadets. The privilege placed him within the ranks of a small and well-respected group of cadets in West Point's history, among whom was Robert E. Lee.

Soon after beginning his West Point education in 1882, Pershing distinguished himself for his devotion, precision, and commanding personality. His classmates (seen here) rewarded Pershing by electing him class president.

During the years Pershing attended the military academy, Civil War veterans made regular visits to West Point. One person often seen at the academy was aging General William Tecumseh Sherman, one of the Union's greatest Civil War leaders. Other visitors also excited the recruits, including the famous writer Mark Twain, who lived in neighboring Connecticut. When Twain—who had grown up in Missouri—discovered that a Missouri boy was at West Point, he paid a call to Pershing's room, told amusing stories to a gathering of cadets, and even called Pershing a "fellow Missourian."

At last, on June 11, 1886, after four difficult but fulfilling years, Pershing graduated as leader of his class. Yet another legendary Civil War general, cavalry commander Phil Sheridan, was the featured speaker at the graduation. After

The Lighter Moments at West Point

For a young man in his late teens or early twenties, four years of difficult study and frequent harassment would be difficult to endure. Even though he was few years older than the average cadet, John Pershing certainly experienced grueling challenges during his time at the school. Even so, life at the academy was not without its laughs and good times.

Many cadets enjoyed an occasional game of baseball or football. Another popular "sport" was pillow fighting. Pershing's classmates gained a reputation as highly skilled pillow fighters who would challenge anyone and everyone to a face-off, which often sent feathers flying. Sometimes such antics ended with upperclassmen ordering those involved to walk around the parade ground, picking up stray feathers. In addition to pillow fighting, cadets played tricks and practical jokes on one another constantly. They worked hard not to get caught, since they might face severe punishments and receive demerits, as well.

In a letter written 25 years after graduation, middle-aged Pershing referred to some of the high times at West Point. During his first guard duty as a plebe, Pershing recalled that several upperclassmen, covered with bed sheets and pretending to be ghosts, approached him in the dark. All Pershing could think to do was cry out to the one closest to him, "Halt, who comes there?" When that "ghost" stopped and stood still, Pershing followed up with, "Halt, who stands there?" Drawing up a nearby chair, the disguised cadet sat himself down, still under his sheet. Pershing then asked the obvious: "Halt, who sits there!?"*

Pershing was not above breaking the rules of the academy, which put him in awkward spots from time to time. One evening after lights out, he was studying French under a blanket to hide the light of his lamp from the prying eyes of upperclassmen. When Pershing and his roommate heard footsteps in the hall, they moved quickly. The roommate hid under a bed as Pershing doused the light and jumped into his own bed completely clothed. When the curious upperclassman broke into the room, he lifted the covers, found Pershing fully dressed, cited him for a rules infraction, and ordered him to carry out a half dozen extra guard duties as punishment.

* Quoted in Richard O'Connor, *Black Jack Pershing.* Garden City, NY: Doubleday & Company, Inc., 1961, p. 26.

four years of wearing cadet gray, the new graduates had earned the privilege of putting on the blue uniform of the U.S. army. As he received his diploma, Pershing had to make a crucial decision. Never intending to be a professional soldier, he had suddenly become one. With his high class standing, Pershing could pick the branch of service he preferred: infantry, cavalry, or artillery. There was never a question about which one he believed held the most prestige. It would be the cavalry for newly graduated John Joseph Pershing.

3

In the Army

During the two days after graduation, the graduates settled their debts at the academy, packed up their belongings, and prepared to leave. By June 14, the class of 1886 went down the Hudson River and attended a grand celebration dinner at New York City's swanky Martinelli's restaurant. The next day, they went sightseeing, clambering up the steps of the city's tallest buildings, visiting the Eden Wax Museum, and walking across the newly constructed Brooklyn Bridge. It was a novel experience for many of the young men, Pershing among them, who wrote later how they "walked across feeling quite shaky." [20] The second evening, the new West Point grads shared another fancy meal, this time at Delmonico's. It was the last time the graduates of the

After graduating from West Point in 1886, Pershing (standing at far left in this portrait) returned to his family, who had relocated to Nebraska. After a brief stay, he received his first cavalry assignment — at Fort Bayard in a desolate part of southwestern New Mexico.

class of 1886 would all be together. By the next day, they began to catch trains, bound for their homes. Some of the graduates, including Pershing, took a side trip to Washington, D.C., to take in the capital's sights. By June 24, though, even Pershing had boarded a train for home.

During his tenure at West Point, Pershing's family had finally abandoned northern Missouri to look for better opportunities. His father had come to believe the economic future of the Laclede area had peaked, and he moved the family to Lincoln, Nebraska.

Over several weeks, Pershing was reunited with the family he had barely seen for four years. Home life was different now. Pershing was a man who had already faced countless rigors and tests. His military career, full of unknown possibilities, lay ahead of him. By early fall, he went to Omaha, Nebraska, where he met other members of his class who were leaving for their posts across the American West.

Second Lieutenant John Pershing's first cavalry assign-ment was at Fort Bayard, situated in the desolate desert hill country of southwest New Mexico. It was one of several army posts in New Mexico at that time, including Forts Union, Wingate, Sumner, Craig, Stanton, as well as Fort Bliss, just over the Texas border near El Paso. Fort Bayard was one of the western outposts where units of the 6th cavalry were stationed. Approximately 300 troops were housed within a quadrangle of buildings that included officers' and enlisted men's barracks, officers' buildings, a commissary, and stables.

One of Pershing's first duties was to establish a string of heliographic stations that could send Morse code messages by reflecting the sun off a mirror. The system was intended to create a communication system between Bayard and Fort Stanton, nearly 100 miles (161 kilometers) to the east. Soon, Pershing had slipped into a daily routine of life at a western army post, which included drills, weapons practice, and riding. Only one month after his arrival, he and his Troop L were sent out in search of a group of raiding Apache Indians who had left their New Mexico reservation.

Although many troops stationed in the West in the 1880s complained of boredom, there was no such problem at Bayard. When the troops were not busy defending U.S. interests in the region, there was an endless parade of activities, including card games, musicales and amateur theater productions, and dances. Life at the fort was a curious mixture of dust and dirt along with certain formalities that made camp life more civilized. For an evening banquet, soldiers would be decked out in dress uniforms and the officers' wives finely dressed in ballgowns. Everyone would eat off imported china, and expensive silverware would be laid out on a table with "red candlesticks and nuts or ferns in silver centerpiece and several forks at the placings, and potted palms in the room corners."[21] On the other hand, nature made life hard at Fort Bayard as those stationed at the fort faced grueling heat in summer and freezing temperatures in winter.

It was at Fort Bayard that Pershing first saw American Indians. It was because of them that the fort existed, and they were a constant part of army life in the West. His memories of the American Indians remained vivid throughout his life. He recalled watching Indian hunters following deer while wearing antlers on their own heads. Perhaps his clearest memory in later years was of a skirmish with some Apache during which a warrior struck Pershing with a tomahawk, knocking him off his horse. The dazed Pershing soon found the Apache standing over him, preparing to scalp him. At the last second, the warrior changed his mind, choosing instead to steal Pershing's revolver, then escape on foot.

Despite this incident, Pershing enjoyed spending time with Indians, talking with them, hearing their stories, and watching them dance. Although many stories he had heard as a child depicted Indians as bloodthirsty savages, Pershing became quite comfortable with those who lived near Fort Bayard. In time, he became adept at negotiating with them. In his book, *Until the Last Trumpet Sounds*, historian Gene

A Brush With Death in the Desert

During Pershing's stint at Fort Bayard, he and a comrade made a personal trip to the Grand Canyon that almost resulted in their deaths in the Arizona desert. In the summer of 1887, Pershing and a fellow trooper, First Lieutenant John Stotsenberg, set out from Fort Wingate, north of Pershing's post, on the 200-mile (322-kilometer) venture. They were accompanied by a mule packer and a Navajo guide named Sam. The first leg of the trip included visiting Zuñi sites and enjoying the eerie and unique Southwestern landscape. They crossed the Oraibi Mountains and the Snake and Dog valleys, riding along lofty mesas and amid brushy desert lands.

On their way to the Grand Canyon, Sam's horse went lame and the guide left to find a replacement. He never returned, and Pershing and Stotsenberg were left to fend for themselves. Almost immediately, things began to go wrong. Their water supply ran low and they lost the trail, leaving the anxious troopers to "wander through canyons and high ridges in brutal sun."* After several days, their mule packer abandoned them, desperate for water. As Pershing and Stotsenberg plodded on in the unfamiliar desert, they began to feel the effects of a lack of water. Their lips and tongues swelled and turned black. Stotsenberg nearly collapsed, but Pershing splashed his face and chest with whiskey, reviving him. It was only a temporary solution. Between them, they only had a cup of water left.

Thinking they were near death, the two lost troopers began to throw away everything they felt they did not need, including Pershing's Winchester rifle. Just when they thought hope was lost, they spotted someone in the distance — Sam, their Navajo guide. He had water and saved the two dying men. The party later found their packer, as well, who had nearly gone mad with thirst. The foursome did eventually reach the famous canyon and, after their return to the safety of their frontier fort, Stotsenberg made an observation with which Pershing could not argue: "We felt that we knew how *not to go* to the Grand Canyon."**

* Quoted in Gene Smith, *Until the Last Trumpet Sounds: The Life and Times of John J. Pershing*, vol. 1. College Station: Texas A & M University Press, 1977, p. 34.

** Ibid.

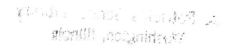

Smith recounts Pershing's capacity for handling relations with the local natives:

> He was very good at dealing with Indians, and had an openness and honesty and earnest willingness to learn and know and understand not seen in soldiers and officers who felt what they considered savages to be a step above animals, but a step below human. . . . By parleying with the chiefs he got the job done, no shooting, no blood. Near Fort Wingate some cattle thieves killed a Zuñi [Indian] and tried to run off a herd to end up besieged along with guiltless cowboys by scores of warriors from the dead man's tribe. Pershing came with ten troopers and brought the trapped men away, managing through diplomacy rather than fighting to get the cowboys freed and the thieves to justice.[22]

Yet even as Pershing tried to treat Indians fairly, he was not beyond taking a firm military stance against them when he felt the situation called for it. Nevertheless, for the young man from Missouri, his days of dealing with the Apache gave him an empathy for their plight, which he later wrote was "mainly the result of government neglect and insincerity." In his opinion, the story of the Indians was "the most cruel, unjust, blackest page of American history."[23]

Although desert duty was not something every cavalry trooper enjoyed, Pershing seems to have taken to the task. Bayard was only one of his assigned posts. He also served at Fort Wingate and Fort Stanton. However, after a few years of shuttling from one New Mexican post to another, he asked for a transfer. Before he was removed from duty in the West in 1890, though, his unit of the 6th cavalry was called to South Dakota, where a mysterious movement was spreading among the Lakota Indians. During the summer and fall of that year, Wovoka, a Paiute medicine man from Nevada, claimed to see visions of God bringing back to the

American Indians everything they had lost as white people encroached on their traditional lands, including the nearly vanished buffalo, good hunting, and plenty of food for their families to eat. Wovoka also said he saw the evacuation of whites from Indian lands. His message spread widely across the West, accompanied by the so-called Ghost Dance, which promised to bring all dead Indians of the past back to life. Some white people misunderstood this mystical activity as a war dance, and the army was called.

By December 1890, Pershing and his fellow troops reached Rapid City, South Dakota, by train. The frontier town was just west of the Pine Ridge Reservation, where Indians were engaging in the Ghost Dance and gathering in increasing numbers. The weather was blistering cold, and the men of the 6th cavalry were issued buffalo overcoats, heavy felt-lined arctic boots, and muskrat caps.

Within a week of Pershing's arrival in Rapid City, Lakota Chief Sitting Bull was shot and killed by Indian police. The 6th cavalry was then sent out to take positions along a ridge of hills, where they were supposed to keep additional Indians from entering Pine Ridge. They were under orders to look out for Chief Big Foot, leader of a large band of Miniconjou Indians and one of the most important chiefs in the region.

Taking up positions along the Cheyenne River between the Pine Ridge Badlands and the Black Hills to the west, Pershing and his fellow troops worked valiantly just to stay warm around wind-blown campfires. For days, they remained in position, witnessing little but the cold, snow, and ceaseless wind of the northern Great Plains. Then, one day, Pershing spotted a prairie-grass fire in the distance. His commander had informed the men that such fires were a sign of an impending Indian attack, but no assault came. Even as the men of the 6th cavalry kept an eye open for Big Foot, the chief walked into the Pine Ridge Reservation at

Wounded Knee Creek to turn himself and his people in. On December 29, the U.S. army's 7th cavalry surrounded the ragged bands of Indians at Wounded Knee, and after the Indians refused to give up their rifles, opened fire, killing 200 Indians, including Big Foot. Pershing's unit did not take part in—or even know about—the lopsided fight.

Three days later, Pershing did see some Indian fighting, however. On January 1, 1891, the 6th cavalry's supply wagons came under attack by a group of Lakota warriors. Quickly, the wagons circled, and the troops prepared for a fight. As the Indians advanced, shots were fired. Several miles away, Pershing and the troops heard the shots and drove their horses over six miles (ten kilometers) of rolling prairie ridges toward the action. When they arrived, Chief War Eagle was ordering his warriors to make an assault. Dashing down the final hill, the men of the 6th cavalry fired their guns as they swept into the valley on horseback, sending the attackers into retreat. It was the only fighting Pershing would see during the Ghost Dance campaign.

The campaign marked the last days Pershing was stationed on the western frontier. He had served four years in New Mexico, and his final months were spent among the newly defeated tribes of the Great Plains. It was time for a change. Pershing had first considered a transfer in 1888, when he applied to the University of Nebraska Board of Regents for a post as an instructor of military tactics. The application had never received a response. During the summer of 1891, he sent another letter, asking for assignment at the university, since he knew a vacancy was coming up in September. His letter mentioned his service in New Mexico and, more recently, his days in the Dakotas where he had been given command of a unit of Sioux scouts. He also said that his family, until recently, had lived in Lincoln. His father and mother had moved to Chicago in 1890, where John Fletcher took another job in sales. Other

After serving four years at various forts in New Mexico, Pershing's 6ᵗʰ cavalry was called to South Dakota to respond to a growing movement among the Native American tribes. Believing that the "Ghost Dance" practiced by the Lakota was a prelude to uprising, the government summoned soldiers to the region to quell any rebellion.

members of the family remained behind in Lincoln, including John Joseph's younger brother, James. Because James had helped Nebraska's secretary of state get elected, his political connections helped him get his brother the appointment at the university that he wanted so dearly.

By late September, John Joseph was a professor of military science and tactics at the University of Nebraska. Pershing found that the university's students had little interest in military training. Many saw no purpose in going into the military. They believed, as Pershing had during his days at West Point, that the possibility that the United States would become involved in a war was remote. The program Pershing came to lead was a poor one. He described finding "a few men, the interest in the battalion weak, the discipline next to nothing, and the instincts of the faculty and the President of the University against the Corps."[24]

Still, Pershing was determined to make the best of the situation. He quickly tightened discipline among his cadets. During the first few weeks, if they showed up for drill with their shoes unpolished, Pershing ordered them to correct that detail before returning.

In addition to teaching military courses, he requested that he be permitted to teach a mathematics course. He also asked if he could take law courses at the university. These requests were granted. Despite his strong attachment to the military, Pershing was still intent on getting a law degree. Soon, 31-year-old Pershing was busy with academic work, both as instructor and student. University life agreed with him. Just as his personality had won him many friends and the attention of his superiors at West Point, Pershing became well known and well liked at the university, especially among the faculty. He attended social gatherings and won a reputation as a wonderful dancer, although he made a point of not dancing with the same girl twice at any gathering.

Before long, Pershing was adding more and more young students to the cadet corps program. He drilled them rigorously, stressed discipline, and encouraged them to engage in regular rifle practice, one of his better skills from his days of Missouri hunting. In his second year at the University of Nebraska, he sent one of his companies to the interstate competitive drill. His cadets called themselves the Pershing Rifles. Despite the fact that well-established programs from some of the best schools in the country were among the competitors, the Pershing Rifles won, bringing the silver cup, along with $1,500 in prize money, back to their school. Such successes had everyone on campus talking about Pershing and his military program. One campus advocate said of Pershing: "He could take a body of cornfed yokels and with only three hours of drill a week turn them into fancy cadets, almost indistinguishable from West Pointers."[25] Often, Pershing was affectionately called "lieut" (pronounced *loot*), short for his rank of second lieutenant.

Success followed the man from Missouri at every turn. After his first year at the university, he was promoted to first lieutenant in the 10th cavalry. Pershing completed his law degree in 1893. His decision to leave the school at the end of his four years at the university saddened many of the faculty, students, and administrators on campus. His tenure at the university was summed up in a letter written by the Nebraska Chancellor, James H. Canfield, who lavished praise on Pershing, saying, "I speak with both experience and observation . . . when I say without the slightest reserve that he is the most energetic, active and industrious, competent and successful I have ever known in a position of this kind." He added, "We have the second best corps of cadets in the United States according to the reports of the United States inspectors; the first being the corps at West Point. Lieutenant Pershing made the corps what it is today."[26]

When his cadets discovered that their beloved instructor was leaving them, their disappointment was keen. Several wanted to make special badges or emblems that they could wear to note their service under Pershing. They approached him and asked for a pair of his uniform trousers. Pershing answered incredulously, "Good Lord! What do you want of my trousers?" They told him of their plan to cut the pants into small pieces so that the blue material and a strip of the yellow border would be included in a badge for each cadet. Pershing surrendered to them one of his best pairs of pants. One student later recalled the tribute: "We made the badges, which as far as I know were the first service badges ever used in the United States."[27] Another student explained why Pershing was so admired and loved by his university cadets: "He did not require of others what he did not require of himself."[28]

In October 1895, three years after he advanced in rank

After serving briefly as a teacher of military tactics at the University of Nebraska, Pershing returned to the West. Nicknamed "Buffalo Soldiers," the African-American troops of the 10th cavalry under Pershing's command found him to be a stern but fair leader.

to first lieutenant, John Pershing returned to duty in the West. Before taking the new post, Pershing had decided not to leave military service and practice law, after all. This time, he served with the 10th cavalry at Fort Assinniboine, Montana, where he remained for a year. The 10th cavalry was a unit of African-American troops under white officers. American Indians referred to these dark-skinned, blue-clad troops as "Buffalo Soldiers," since their skin color reminded the Indians of the shade of bison hides. As usual, Pershing proved a stern commander. Historian Gene Smith sums up Pershing's command of the 10th cavalry: "Racial matters did not appear of great interest or import to Lieutenant Pershing. It was efficiency that counted."[29] Behind his back, Pershing's men affectionately called him "Old Red," because of the color of his hair.

Among Pershing's duties during his Montana stint was the return of hundreds of Cree Indians who had slipped across the Canadian border into the American West. When he delivered the Cree to Canadian authorities, one of the warriors, who was wanted for the murder of a Canadian priest, shot himself and committed suicide. The bullet that left his body whizzed close by Pershing himself.

By December 17, 1896, Pershing had been reassigned to duties at the headquarters of the army in Washington, D.C. His work often kept him tied to a desk, which he did not enjoy, and after only six months, he was back at Fort Assinniboine. He did not remain there long, however. A position for an instructor in military tactics opened up at West Point. Pershing won the appointment and was assigned duty at West Point on June 15, 1897. The job lasted only a year, but the experience proved difficult for Pershing. The cadets of West Point came to hate him.

During those months at West Point, Pershing was remembered for his rigidity. Perhaps being back at his old alma mater, under the watchful eye of the very instructors who had taught him, Pershing felt he had something to prove. He was unrelenting. The following provides a description of his behavior:

> To his charges he seemed a heartless martinet, rigid, unfor-
> giving, always ready to pounce on the slightest departure
> from perfect performance, someone seeming ever ready —
> indeed anxious — to mark down demerits. The cadets
> detested him . . . [and] they made their feelings entirely clear.
> . . . Pershing was silenced. It was done in the most public and
> humiliating fashion. When he entered the vast mess hall an
> instant noiselessness seized the corps of cadets. No one
> moved a muscle as he went to his table. So palpable a display
> of hatred could well destroy a career, for knowledge and
> mention of it could be expected to follow an officer always.[30]

Pershing's response to such behavior was to ignore it and continue to hand out demerits, so circumstances did not improve. Cadets came up with a long list of cruel nicknames: Farmer John, Wooden Willy, the Widow's Mite, and Black Jack, for his having commanded the Buffalo Soldiers of the 10th cavalry.

Besides problems with the cadets, there were other frustrations for Pershing at West Point. When he tried to approach the academy's commander about possible changes in the curriculum, so that it might better equip army officers for the swiftly approaching twentieth century, he was ignored. His first semester teaching at West Point was filled with difficulties and rejection. As the second semester began at the start of 1898, however, Pershing would soon face a series of events that would abruptly change his future. Those events would lead the United States into the ultimate clash of arms—war with Spain.

4

Action in Cuba

Since the mid-1890s, political events had been simmering in the tropical heat of the Caribbean on the Spanish colonial island of Cuba. A popular revolution called *Cuba Libre* ("Free Cuba") had challenged the continued power of Spain over the Cuban people. In 1896, the U.S. Congress, sympathetic to the cause of Cuban independence, passed a resolution recognizing the Cubans' right to rebel against Spain. Over the next two years, Americans showed increasing support for U.S. military intervention on the side of the Cubans. This view was trumpeted by American newspapers, which were eager for a war with Spain, since a war would dramatically increase readership. Despite the popular outcry, the newly elected president, Republican William McKinley, was intent on avoiding war.

In February 1898, the U.S. battleship *Maine* exploded in the harbor at Havana, Cuba. American press reports fueled the belief that the Spanish were behind the ship's sinking — leading Congress to declare war on Spain. Pershing, who had been unhappily serving as a teacher at West Point, would at last see combat.

A news-hungry American public received reports of Spanish atrocities against the Cuban people, including the burning of villages and the internment of thousands of Cuban peasants in concentration camps, where starvation and disease killed hundreds of victims. Americans grew more angry with each story of Spanish mistreatment of the Cubans. Then, in February 1898, the U.S. battleship *Maine* exploded mysteriously while docked in the harbor at Havana, Cuba. The tragic destruction of the vessel sparked a new outburst of war fever among the American public. President McKinley could no longer ignore the cries for intervention and, in late April, he asked Congress to declare war against Spain. Suddenly, the American military was at war at a time when the U.S. army had only 28,000 men in uniform. Among these soldiers was First Lieutenant John J. Pershing.

Pershing was more than ready to leave his post at West Point. He had written to a friend in February about his frustrations at the academy, stating, "I have gotten out of this about all there is in it."[31] That April, with war on the horizon, he wrote to the assistant secretary of war, an old associate and former Nebraska representative George Meiklejohn, requesting reassignment to the 10th cavalry: "I would not miss service in the field for anything. . . . I have existed all these years in the service for just this sort of thing and . . . if I should accept any duty which would keep me from field service . . . I should never forgive myself."[32] He asked Meiklejohn, "May I be relieved from here? George, I could no more keep out of the field than I could fly."[33] Meiklejohn pulled some strings in Washington, D.C., and Pershing gained his transfer. He received orders to catch up with the 10th cavalry in Georgia. Pershing was soon back in service with the 10th cavalry, which had already been chosen to go to Cuba and fight the Spanish.

Most Americans, both civilian and military, had no doubt that the United States would defeat Spain in this war for the liberation of Cuba. The nation was filled with confidence and righteous might. Not many people were worried that fewer than 20,000 American soldiers would engage as many as 80,000 Spanish troops already on the island. Americans felt the cause was just and that U.S. soldiering would prove superior.

By mid-May, the 10th cavalry reached Lakeland, Florida, where troops, horses, pack mules, equipment, and supplies were crowded together, all awaiting shipment to

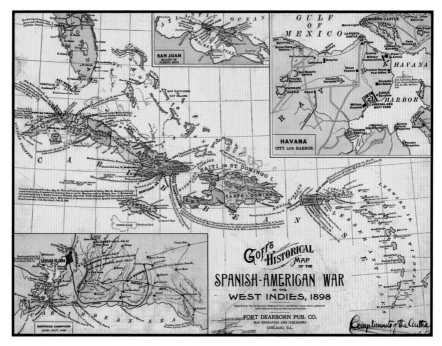

As this map shows, fighting an island war is a complicated affair. Still, even though American troops were outnumbered nearly four to one by Spanish forces, few doubted that the United States would emerge victorious.

Cuba. After several delays, Pershing and his men were onboard southbound transports by June 14 and reached Cuban waters in just a few days. During the short voyage, Pershing became emotional about what he and thousands of American soldiers were about to do. He wrote in a letter, "There will never sail from our shores a finer body of men than we have right here."[34]

The landing of the 10th cavalry on the Cuban coast took place on June 23. At the same time, other landings were taking place at additional sites along the Cuban coast. The ultimate inland target was the city of Santiago. The target date for taking the city was July 1. After landing, the various units of cavalry were brought together. Their horses were pushed out of each ship's cargo openings and left to swim to shore. Some, however, swam out to sea and were never seen again. The heat was stifling as the men landed, wearing army-issue woolen uniforms. Back in Florida, Pershing had been very anxious to get to Cuba, afraid he might miss the action. He later wrote, "everybody was so eager to go and so fearful of being left behind at the last moment that almost any conditions would have been accepted without grumbling."[35] Those eager attitudes did not last long after U.S. troops reached their destination.

The overall commander of the American forces was Brigadier General William Rufus Shafter, 63 years old and a portly 300 pounds. The cavalry commander was Joseph Wheeler, who had ridden as a Confederate cavalry officer during the Civil War and earned the nickname "Fighting Joe." Pershing was excited about the 10th cavalry's assignment alongside Theodore Roosevelt's troops. When the war broke out, Roosevelt, a future president of the United States, was serving as assistant secretary of the U.S. navy. He immediately resigned his post and helped form a unique group of volunteers that included old friends from his student days at Harvard University, fellow polo players, cowboys he knew from his days as a rancher in North Dakota, as well as some American Indians. Once his 1st volunteer cavalry, called the "Rough Riders," was pieced together, Roosevelt did everything he could to make certain his unit reached Cuba in time to fight.

On June 30, U.S. forces, including two infantry divisions, two squadrons of Rough Riders, the 10th cavalry, and a squadron of the 1st cavalry, were within sight of two hills—San Juan and Kettle. The hills were part of the strategic perimeter of defenses laid down by the Spanish to halt the American advance on Santiago. Shafter and his subordinates held a council and discussed their plan. They decided that one infantry division, under the command of Brigadier General H.W. Lawton, would advance on a hacienda (large estate) called El Caney, up in the heights. As soon as his men broke enemy resistance, the second infantry division would advance to San Juan Heights. Lawton's men would then join the main assault on the hills that were directly in the army's path to Santiago. The cavalry, including Pershing's 10th, would take part in the assault.

As the battle opened early that morning, the American forces were soon pinned down by withering fire from hundreds of well-entrenched and well-hidden Spanish riflemen. The cavalrymen, including Pershing, were under orders to wait to advance until the infantry had successfully forced out Spanish resistance. The infantry assault, however, became mired down by poor leadership and deadly fire from Spanish sharpshooters. After several hours, the slow pace of the assault was broken when frustrated officers in the field, angered by their lack of progress, ignored their immediate orders and chose to lead their men forward. Those forces that fought their way through a hail of Spanish bullets included those led by John Pershing. As he and other commanders drove their men forward, Kettle Hill soon fell into American hands.

With multiple units gathered on Kettle Hill, now in open country and out of the menacing jungle, American firepower could effectively target the Spanish riflemen who had plagued them for hours. For the first time that day, American rifles laid down a devastating sheet of fire — 3,600 rounds a minute — against the entrenched Spanish in the distance. Historian Frank Vandiver describes the shifting fortunes of the furious battle:

> With the new American scything at the top of the hill, some of the defenders quit the field. Now the view of the hillside changed; up out of the grass came the Yanks, in campaign hats cocked and dirty, their rifles glinting. As U.S. artillery joined in support, these figures began to run upward, some tumbling, spinning down, the rest surging on, bayonets

flashing—and over the scene came a curious, high-pitched yelling. . . . No one ordered a battle yell and it was not disciplined, but it was terrible and chilling and it bubbled in the blood.

A last rush came after a short halt to let U.S. shells search further uphill. When the barrage lifted, the whole line stormed the crest and the enemy. San Juan Hill belonged to the takers.[36]

One of those "takers" was John J. Pershing. Another was Theodore Roosevelt, whose Rough Riders had been in the thick of the action that resulted in the taking of San Juan Hill. This single military advance would make Roosevelt a hero

An Early Meeting

Pershing and Roosevelt had met once before the war, back in January 1897. While on his second stint out in Montana with the 10th cavalry, Pershing had been sent to New York City for a military tournament. There, he met up with an old friend from his West Point class, Avery Andrews, who invited Pershing to join him for dinner. A second guest at the evening meal was then–New York Police Commissioner Theodore Roosevelt.

Separated in age by only two years, Pershing and Roosevelt had mixed well that evening. They talked about their experiences out west (Roosevelt had owned a ranch in the Dakotas during the 1880s), including geography, American Indians, and hunting. When the evening was over, Pershing and Roosevelt parted, impressed with one another. Then, by the summer of 1898, they were serving nearly side by side in Cuba during the advance against the Spanish-held city of Santiago.

Roosevelt would remember Pershing in later years, particularly from Pershing's efforts during the El Caney battle. When Roosevelt became president, he made serious efforts to help advance Pershing's military career. The two men developed a relationship based on mutual admiration and respect.

Pershing was not the only military man whose career would be furthered by the Spanish-American War. In leading his "Rough Riders" in the taking of San Juan Hill, a young Theodore Roosevelt began to build the reputation for leadership that would one day earn him a place in the White House.

back home and help launch his career to new heights, including election as President McKinley's second vice president in 1900 and a rise to the presidency following McKinley's assassination just ten months later.

The adrenaline-charged Pershing had survived the battle and led his troops well. As the battle wound down, he looked about with concern for his comrades, helped several of the wounded, and examined the field for lingering enemy shooters. Pershing was immediately proud of his African-American troops and their tenacity in the battle. "We officers of the Tenth Cavalry could have taken our black heroes in our arms," he later remembered.[37]

After the capture of San Juan and Kettle hills, as well as other advances made by American forces, Spanish resistance in Santiago did not last long. Spirited fighting continued the next two days, and one of Pershing's best friends in uniform, Mal Barnum, was seriously wounded. On July 3, the Spanish fleet anchored in Santiago attempted to flee the island for open seas, but the out-of-date, heavy Spanish ships were blasted by the guns of the U.S. navy. By July 4, the Spanish had surrendered. Although fighting continued for a short time in the Philippines, the Spanish-American War in Cuba, one of America's shortest military engagements, was over. As for the men of the 10th cavalry, their casualty figures were significant. In his report, Pershing revealed that 18 percent of the regiment had been killed or wounded; half the officers were also casualties.

In the aftermath of the fighting, Pershing received much praise from his superiors, both for his actions during combat and his persistence in working to keep his men supplied in the field. Supplies, including food, were not delivered regularly, and Pershing's men suffered accordingly. Pershing, however, was able to find supplies here and take there, bypassing regulations that required requisition forms. "He appropriated mules and wagons without requisition, clothing, blanket rolls, such extra food as was available. The Tenth suffered, as did all Americans in Cuba, but less than others."[38] An admiring superior told Pershing: "You did some tall rustling and if you had not we would have starved, as none of the others were able or strong enough to do it."[39] These well-intended efforts caused Pershing to bend rules, as he had never allowed himself to do during his previous twelve years in active military service. The war in Cuba shook loose some of Pershing's rigidity.

For his bravery under fire, Pershing won additional praise. A captain noted, "The gallantry you displayed under fire and the untiring energy you evinced, were a devotion to duty exceeded by none, and equaled by few."[40] For his "gallantry in action against the Spanish forces, July 1, 1898," Pershing received the Silver Star. In the official report about the attack on Santiago, Pershing was named for his "untiring energy, faithfulness and gallantry."[41] Colonel Theodore Baldwin proposed a brevet commission for Pershing. In a letter written to the Missouri hero, Baldwin added, "I have been in many fights and through the Civil War, but on my word 'You were the coolest and bravest man I ever saw under fire in my life' and carried out your orders to the letter—no matter where it called you."[42] As a result of his brief but difficult tour in Cuba, John Pershing was promoted to the rank of major in the volunteer army.

5

Assignments in Paradise

F ollowing his service in the Spanish-American War, Pershing's military career, then 12 years removed from his days as a student at West Point, began to accelerate dramatically. Pershing did not return to West Point to teach. Instead, he was assigned to a desk position in Washington, D.C. His duties in the nation's capital included organizing the Insular Bureau, an office established to administer the territory ceded to the United States by Spain as a result of the war, including the former Spanish colonies of Cuba, Puerto Rico, and the Pacific island group of the Philippines. The office job did not suit the veteran field commander. By the summer of 1899, Filipino revolutionaries were fighting against American control of their

After the Spanish-American War, Pershing's military career began to accelerate. In 1899, he traveled to the Philippines to face a group of Muslim revolutionaries who challenged America's control of the islands. Combining earnest diplomacy with brutal military efficiency, Pershing was able to subdue the rebellion.

lands just as they had done earlier against the Spanish. Pershing saw an opportunity for action in the Pacific. He requested a transfer to the Philippines.

His Philippine adventure began with a tour of Europe. Pershing sailed first to England, where he took an official tour of the Woolwich Arsenal. In France, he walked the halls of the Louvre and the palace of seventeenth-century monarch Louis XIV, at Versailles. He soaked in the art of Italy, sailed to Egypt, then through the Indian Ocean to Sri Lanka, southeast of India. He reached the Filipino capital of Manila in November 1899, having seen much of the world. He had come a long way from his boyhood days in north-central Missouri.

Upon his arrival in the Pacific, Pershing took up duties as adjutant general of the Filipino districts of Mindanao and

Jolo. Soon, he was caught up in the exotic world of the East, finding "the sky fascinating in line and color. The East of strange aromas, outlines of the distance quivering in the heat—the Orient and Asia and the tropics seized him, never to relax its grip. John Pershing was never bored in the Philippines."[43]

Despite his love of the beauty of the Philippines, Pershing faced daunting responsibilities from the first day of his arrival. The western Mindanao hills were home to 100,000 warlike Moros, a rebellious Muslim people who had never been fully subjugated by the Spanish over the previous three centuries. The Moros were fiercely independent, operating in autonomous bands and ruled by sultans. It became Pershing's primary task to subdue the Moros, who were developing a hatred for the Americans just as they had for the Spanish.

By 1901, Pershing was promoted to a captain's rank in the regular army. For nearly two years, he met with several key Moro leaders, who were as polite and civil to him as he was to them. Despite many Moro fears and exaggerations about Americans, Pershing was seen by nearly all as a man of his word, one to be trusted, yet one who was capable of telling them directly what he wanted from them. They came to see him as very different from any of the other outsiders with whom they had ever dealt. As a first lieutenant with the 15th cavalry explained, "They regard him as a supernatural being. He always treats them fairly, never makes a promise which he cannot fulfill."[44]

The Moros may have accepted Pershing himself, but two chiefs still refused to agree to peace terms, since they deeply resented the presence of American troops at Mindanao. The Moros' harassment of the American military camps finally forced Pershing to lead troops, in April 1903, against the strongly belligerent sultan of

Bacleod, the most important of the Moro chiefs. Refusing to surrender their arms, 600 Moro fanatics occupied a fortress in the hill country of Lake Lanao. Pershing attacked the stronghold and defeated them. This action successfully ended the Moro rebellion against the United States, representing a singular military and diplomatic coup for Pershing.

By 1903, Pershing's first assignment in the Philippines was over. He was recalled to Washington, where he was installed as a member of the General Staff Corps as a reward for his successes, both diplomatic and military, with the Moros. He remained with the corps until 1906. Those three years were eventful for Pershing, who was then in his early forties. For a time, Pershing served as the U.S. military attaché in Tokyo, Japan; he reported to his superiors on the war being fought between the Japanese and the Russians through 1904–1905, a war that President Roosevelt helped end through negotiations. Roosevelt's efforts won him the Nobel Peace Prize.

During his first year back in service in Washington, Pershing surprised nearly everyone who had ever known him by falling deeply in love with a woman almost half his age. The woman was 23-year-old Helen Frances Warren, whose friends and family called her "Frankie." She was the daughter of Senator Francis Emroy Warren from Cheyenne, Wyoming, one of the state's richest men. A graduate of Wellesley College, she was vivacious and cultured, yet unpretentious. She was described as "tall, filled with energy and go, jolly . . . unspoiled despite her father's . . . financial status. . . . No one ever truthfully called Frankie Warren beautiful. But she had a good, kind face, was likable, and had the most delightful laugh."[43]

Frankie Warren was aware of Pershing's reputation as a soldier and diplomat even before she met him. While attending a Capitol luncheon in early December, President

Following his experiences in the Philippines, Pershing returned to Washington and served under President Theodore Roosevelt (seen here). Soon after, Roosevelt assigned Pershing as military attaché in Tokyo to report on a war that had developed between Japan and Russia. Roosevelt's skilled negotiating helped end the war and earned him a Nobel Peace Prize.

Roosevelt referred to Pershing in a speech. Two days later, Warren went to a dance where Pershing was also in attendance. That night, in her diary, she noted: *"Perfectly lovely time.* Met Mr. Pershing, of Moro and Presidential message fame."[44] The following day, she attended a dinner and saw Pershing there, too. That evening's diary entry told the story: "It was just great. Have lost my heart."[45] The feeling was mutual. Pershing informed an old Nebraska friend: "I've met the girl God made for me!"[46]

Just over a year after their first meeting, Pershing asked Senator Warren for his daughter's hand. Initial plans were made for a June 1905 wedding. Two days after becoming engaged, however, Pershing was informed by Secretary of War William Howard Taft that he was to be assigned as the U.S. military attaché to Tokyo. The wedding date was moved to January 26, and the couple said their vows in Washington's Church of the Epiphany, with the president and the first lady present, along with 4,500 additional guests. They left for Tokyo the following day and sailed for Japan on St. Valentine's Day. Pershing seemed to be happy with his bride, writing, "Love her more and more. She is the dearest girl in the world. And I the happiest man."[47]

Pershing served as military attaché to Japan for nine months. He spent much of his time on tour in Manchuria observing the war between the Japanese and the Russians as closely as possible. His work kept him and Frankie apart for months. Despite his lifelong attraction to the action of war, Pershing longed to be with his wife. "I hope this blooming war will soon end," he wrote in his diary. "I am just as forlorn as I can be."[48] When the war did end, he and Frankie were reunited. In time, the couple had two homes in Japan, including a rented beach house at Hayama, where the two could enjoy some solitude together. From their house, they could see Mount Fuji. Pershing later wrote, "When the moon shone and light breezes rustled through the pines and caused the temple bells to tinkle, my wife and I felt that peace was as near about us as we should ever find it on this earth."[49]

Pershing's personal happiness was suddenly broken when, on March 16, 1906, his father died in Lincoln, Nebraska, at the home of Pershing's sister Mary. During the months that followed, Pershing was racked with guilt and sorrow. He struggled through the summer of 1906 as "Cold, clutching grief stalked the Pershing home."[50] Through those difficult months, the generally stoic officer relied on his young wife for support, which she offered without hesitation. Brighter days were ahead, however. An addition to his own family helped Pershing get over the loss of his father. On September 8, 1906, Frankie gave birth to the Pershings' first child, named for her mother, Helen Frances.

Less than two weeks after the arrival of baby Helen, Pershing received important news from Washington. President Roosevelt had nominated him to the rank of brigadier general. The appointment set off a firestorm of controversy, since it allowed the Missouri veteran to jump ahead of 257 senior captains, 364 majors, 131 lieutenant colonels, and 110 colonels — a total of 862 officers who had been superior in rank to Pershing. Roosevelt's move infuriated people in the War Department. Charges quickly surfaced that Pershing's appointment had been the result of string-pulling by his father-in-law, Senator Warren. Roosevelt addressed such criticisms with a compelling bit of insight: "To promote a man because he married a Senator's daughter would be an infamy; to refuse him promotion for the same reason would be an equal infamy."[51] President Roosevelt refused to withdraw the promotion. Soon, the newly promoted Brigadier General John J. Pershing and his wife were on their way to a new assignment at a Pacific post just as exotic as the one they had enjoyed in the shadow of Mount Fuji.

Bringing along his family, Pershing took command of Fort McKinley, a new U.S. post situated near Manila. Among Pershing's duties was teaching classes to junior officers, including lessons on his observations from the Russo-Japanese War. Camp social life was similar to that at many military outposts of the day. The wives of officers tried to create a world of formal dinners, dances, and other activities:

> Nights after Retreat and the flag-lowering to trumpet and gun salute and turnout of troops, officers wore smart white high-collar tropical uniforms heavily starched and with gilt braid trappings of gold, while the ladies of the garrison were in filmy summer dance frocks or ball gowns. One dined off fine china and ate with good silver; and later, at the potted palm- and long-veranda Army and Navy Club, the band alternated between waltz and two-step. It was always warm, but the high elevation spared residents the greenhouselike steamy and humid heat of the lowlands. . . . The Pershings entertained on a grand scale. When [Secretary of War] William Howard Taft was guest of honor, the centerpiece of the table was in the shape of the White House.[52]

By the summer of 1907, Frankie was pregnant again. Because the temperatures at Fort McKinley were so warm, Pershing sent his wife to another military site, Camp John Hay, up in the mountains where daytime temperatures rarely rose higher than the mid-60s°F. Separation from his wife was difficult for Pershing, who wrote in a letter to her, "Frank, you may think I am a baby or a booby, but I don't care what you think. I simply cannot live without you." Feeling a strong sense of loneliness, the general added, "Damn the service. Damn everything and everybody that takes from me or ever has taken from me one minute of your time or one thought of your mind. . . . Oh, Frances, I need you every moment. I cannot live without you."[53]

Pershing was present when his second child arrived on the night of March 26, 1908. The new baby, another daughter, was named for one of Frankie's close friends, Anne Orr. Everyone noted how she looked like her father, "even to the dimples."[54] Pershing could often be seen standing over baby Anne's bassinet, smiling at his newborn.

Despite his attachment to his family, the general remained an efficient commander, one who always expected his men to perform at their best. Now approaching 50 years of age, however, Pershing was having health problems. He suffered from fevers that had plagued him since his days in Cuba during the Spanish-American War, the leftover reminders of recurring malaria, as well as sprue, which caused anemia. Pershing also began to have heart palpitations. His health became such a worry and source of discomfort that Pershing finally decided he should ask for a transfer at the end of his tour of duty and return to the United States. He had, after all, spent more than a decade assigned to tropical posts.

On a Saturday evening, June 27, 1908, 400 well-wishers gathered at Fort McKinley to see the Pershings off as they prepared to depart the islands. Pershing's Philippine tour "marked a happy time in Pershing's life, eighteen months of accomplishment. . . . And he knew, too, that in the warmth and affection of his good brothers came his fullest achievement—friendship."[55] On the trip home, the family took a tour of Russia, where they visited St. Petersburg and Moscow, taking in the sights, which included many churches with onion domes and "high-booted czarist soldier[s]."[56] In Germany, Pershing visited the German War Office and saw firsthand the extent of the Germany military. From his observations, Pershing determined that "Germany had the finest military machine that had ever existed."[57] Passing through Belgium, Pershing took Frankie on a side trip to see Waterloo, the final battlefield of Napoleon Bonaparte.

Once they reached the United States, Pershing made

The Penniless General

As a general in the U.S. army, Pershing did not have to worry much about the immediate financial needs of his family. His rank provided more than adequate military or government housing and the Pershing household was typically crowded with servants. Frankie was herself independently well-off, and money was rarely an issue of concern. On one occasion, however, Pershing and his family found themselves thousands of miles from home without any money, stranded penniless in a remote corner of Russia.

When the Pershings left their Filipino assignment at Fort McKinley in the summer of 1908, they took the long way home, through Japan, Russia, and Europe. As they reached the Siberian city of Vladivostok, their expenses began to accumulate as they paid a seemingly endless number of carriage drivers, porters, and others to deliver the family luggage and household wares to the local train station. Pershing had difficulty cashing a bank draft drawn on a bank in Washington, D.C. When he finally did cash it, he received the equivalent of $600. Once he bought the family's rail tickets and paid all the baggage handlers and other service people, Pershing had only three Russian rubles — equal to $1.50 — left. Suddenly, he was caught in a crisis. The family had ten days of travel ahead before reaching Moscow and no money for food.

Frankie was worried. For the moment, the nearly penniless General Pershing had no idea what to do. His wife began to cry, and his children were hungry. Aboard a Russian train, the Pershings faced a difficult problem.

For the first time in his life, Pershing would have to beg for help. He remembered seeing a Danish naval officer on the train. Pershing went to his luggage and found a box of fine Filipino cigars. He then went to the officer's compartment, offered him the cigars, and sheepishly told him about the family's plight.

To the Dane, Pershing's story — a U.S. general stranded in the frozen reaches of Siberia — was amusing. Still, he gave Pershing the help he needed, loaning him money to complete his trip. Although Pershing had been forced to ask humbly for help from a total stranger, Pershing later wrote, "Anything was pardonable to save those we love."*

* Quoted in Gene Smith, *Until the Last Trumpet Sounds: The Life and Times of John J. Pershing*, vol. 1. College Station: Texas A & M University Press, 1977, p. 102.

many visits to doctors, in a desperate search for a cure to his ills. A doctor in Germany had told Pershing that he had a heart condition. The army's surgeon general examined Pershing and told him that he should quit smoking. Pershing had smoked since boyhood, and by now, he was consuming a dozen cigars daily. He took the doctor's advice and smoked only rarely for the rest of his life.

With all the attention centered on his disease, Pershing began to decline even more. Historian Frank Vandiver describes Pershing's downward health spiral:

> By then the family had become alarmed. Jack's morale declined rapidly, and he began to act like an invalid. A kind of creeping insecurity circumscribed his daily life, until he lurked almost in seclusion. Utterly unlike him, this melancholia seemed more serious than anything diagnosed by doctors. Fear inspired despair, and Jack felt his first twinge of mortality. He was forty-eight; would he ever again return to duty?[58]

Pershing spent three months at a sanitarium in New York, and followed this period of recuperation with another month at the Army and Navy Hospital in Hot Springs, Arkansas, under the care of a doctor with whom he had graduated from West Point. Major George Deshon examined his friend and finally informed him: "John, we have subjected you to every known test, and in my opinion and in that of my associates there isn't a damn thing the matter with you."[59] Deshon followed up the diagnosis with a suggestion that the two old comrades saddle a couple of horses and take a long ride together the next morning. Once Pershing was in the saddle, he rediscovered the zest for life that had carried him through West Point, through wars, and from one corner of the globe to the other.

For Pershing, it was a turning point. He created a new regimen for himself—"two hours on a horse each day, lots of sleep, a good diet, forty minutes of calisthenic exercises followed by a salt rub, [and] a daily hour nap."[60] He also made plans to return to Manila with his growing family. During Pershing's illness, Frankie had given birth to a boy, named for his grandfather, Francis Warren Pershing. Born June 24, 1909, the baby, who would be called Warren by the family, weighed 12 pounds.

By November 1909, the Pershings were back in the Philippines, where the general had been appointed governor of the Filipino province of Moro, his old post. Slowly, but tenaciously, American military leaders in the Philippines, such as Pershing, had been successful in subduing the more militant factions of Filipino revolutionaries. Even ten years after the Spanish-American War, though, pockets of resistance remained. A lengthy campaign against a band of several hundred diehard holdouts among the more ferocious Moro bands took Pershing into the jungle in search of them, along with 500 American troops and an equal number of Filipino scouts. It was Cuban fighting once again, as "movement of troops was difficult through the jungle, where, in many places, the troops were compelled to cut a pathway, in doing which they were exposed to sudden and fierce attacks by fanatical Moros."[61] It was not until Christmas Day, 1911, that most of the Moro fighters surrendered. Others held out even longer. Following the Battle of Bagsag, fought in June 1913, Moro opposition reached its end. In defeat, the Moros exalted their conqueror, John J. Pershing. They appointed him as a datto, a leader of their tribe.

While Pershing had fought hard to subdue the Moros and other tribal groups, he had also worked to improve the lives of those under the jurisdiction of the United States. The landscape saw modern improvements, including "bridges, ports, warehouses, markets, wagon roads,

In his mid-forties, Pershing fell in love with a woman half his age. Helen Frances Warren, the daughter of a Wyoming senator, became Mrs. Pershing in January 1905—just as Pershing was due to leave for his assignment in Japan. The couple is seen here with three of the four children they would have together.

railroads, and industrial enterprises."[62] He encouraged Filipino farmers to diversify their production of a variety of products, including rubber, sugar, coffee, rice, and cotton. He established dozens of clinics where the native population could receive medical care. Meanwhile, on May 20, 1912, Frankie gave birth to another daughter, Mary Margaret.

By 1913, Pershing's work in the Philippines, an assignment that had begun back in 1899, appeared to be complete. There was very little military action still needed against any native Filipinos. Significant improvements in education, health, and the general welfare of the people had helped develop an endearing trust between the natives and Pershing. Pershing and Frankie had come to appreciate the raw beauty of the tropical paradise and were saddened by the thought of leaving the place where two of their four children had been born. Many of the couple's early roots together had grown from time spent in the Philippines, and now they were leaving.

A Punitive Expedition

The Pershings left their Pacific island home in December 1913, sailing on the army transport *Sherman*, named for the great Union general Pershing remembered from his West Point days. They docked at San Francisco, where the general was to take command of the Presidio, an old military post. Pershing returned from his work in the Pacific as a hero praised in the American press, having subdued the Moros and brought the Filipino people modern conveniences.

The Pershings' new home was not as exotic or spacious as the one they had had in the Philippines, but there was an expansive yard where the children could play. The temperature was also milder, and there were many amusements in the city, which had been completely rebuilt after a devastating earthquake less than ten years earlier. As it turned out, however, Pershing's stint at the Presidio was not destined to be long.

When Pershing took up his duties, American military personnel were already focused on events taking place close to home, in Mexico, where a revolution had been under way for several years. In 1913, Mexican General Victoriano Huerta had taken control of the Mexican government through a coup. Huerta's presidency made Mexico a dictatorship, however, and the U.S. government, with its own newly elected president, Woodrow Wilson, refused to recognize the harsh Huerta regime. Wilson cut off diplomatic relations with Mexico.

Pershing had been following events in Mexico even before he left the Philippines. Events south of the border were bringing Mexico to its knees. Lawlessness reigned, and in the rural countryside, *bandidos* (bandits) felt free to raid Mexican towns and plunder rich and poor alike. Mexico was on the brink of anarchy, and President Wilson was mindful of the proximity of these events to the Mexican-American border. In the Texas border town of El Paso, citizens had piled up mattresses against the windows of their shops and homes in case Mexican bullets strayed across the border. American citizens in Mexico, especially businessmen and diplomats, feared for their lives. Wilson quickly formed an ill opinion of General Huerta, and determined that the revolutionary must someday be removed from power.

Within Mexico itself, opponents of Huerta began to multiply. A new revolution, led by Venustiano Carranza, soon arose. Carranza received support from other revolutionaries, including Doroteo Arango, known popularly as Francisco "Pancho" Villa, and Álvaro Obregón. In northern Mexico, everyone knew the name of Pancho Villa. His followers were usually a ragtag collection of people with little political power, less land ownership, and almost no wealth. Carranza's supporters successfully overthrew Huerta, and occupied Mexico City. Villa, however, soon had a falling out with Carranza because he was not included in the new government. Wilson recognized Carranza's government and vowed to help cut off gun shipments to his enemies, including Villa. To carry out this promise, in April 1914, Pershing was ordered to take two infantry regiments to Fort Bliss, outside El Paso. This time, he left his family behind.

When Pershing arrived in the Texas border town, everyone was concerned about a possible attack by Pancho Villa, even though the Mexican *pistolero* had no intentions of making such a raid on U.S. soil. During the following weeks, Pershing drilled his men and sent them out on border patrols, letting them be seen in border towns to ease the anxiety of U.S. citizens who felt caught in the revolutionary crossfire.

The wild card in the equation along the border was always Pancho Villa. To his supporters, he was the embodiment of the revolutionary spirit, a voice for the poor and landless, someone who was fighting for noble goals while sporting a pair of bullet-filled bandoliers across his chest. To others, he was nothing more than a bandit, an opportunist who was ready to steal to line his own pockets. He visited El Paso from time to time, buying ice cream at a shop called the Elite Confectionery. He even paid a call on Pershing "with revolvers bulging from pants pockets."[63] He and the general had their photograph taken together, along with General Álvaro Obregón. During that first year at Fort Bliss, little changed in Pershing's border-patrol routine.

In the meantime, war had broken out in Europe. In June 1914, a Serbian nationalist had assassinated the heir

In this photograph, an unusually jovial General Pershing (right) meets with Mexican revolutionary Pancho Villa (center) and General Álvaro Obregón (left). Soon after, Pershing would lead his cavalry through Mexico in an unsuccessful pursuit of Villa, who was seen as a threat to Mexico's stability and a menace to U.S. border towns.

to the Austro-Hungarian throne, infuriating the Austrians and their German allies. When Russia moved to support the government of Serbia (which was not implicated in the assassination), Germany had moved for war, deciding to attack the French, an ally of the Russians. The Great War (World War I) was in full course by September as European powers, bound together by a confusing tangle of overlapping military alliances, moved aggressively against their neighbors. For the moment, however, the war was across the ocean, too far away to be considered an American problem.

Pershing, tired of being apart from his family, began to make plans for Frankie and the children to come to live in El Paso. In late July, he received a missive from his dear wife, which ended with sentimental lines, "I love you so

While serving in El Paso, Pershing received the horrifying news that his home in San Francisco (seen here) had burned, with the fire taking the lives of his wife and their three daughters. A devastated Pershing sent his surviving son to live with the boy's aunts in Nebraska.

much—I am getting weary of being away from you. Oh, I love you, dear one!"[64] Pershing could no longer bear the separation. Finally, the family decided to move to El Paso on August 28. Frankie and the girls, however, never made it there.

On the night of August 26, a fire broke out in the Pershing house when coal fell out of the dining room fireplace and ignited the flammable varnish on the wooden floors. Frankie and the three girls—eight-year-old Helen, seven-year-old Anne, and three-year-old Mary Margaret—all died of smoke inhalation. A private stationed at the Presidio went into the burning house and rescued six-year-old Warren, who was found unconscious on the floor of his bedroom.

When Pershing received the tragic news of the deaths of his wife and three daughters, he was devastated. He left El Paso immediately by train for San Francisco. During the ride, he was inconsolable and cried constantly. Upon his arrival, he visited the Clark and Booth Mortuary, where all four bodies were laid out in their coffins. He approached each one and knelt. After an hour, he asked to see his burned-out home. Then, he went to see his son, Warren, at the post hospital. Frankie and the girls were buried in the Warren family plot in Cheyenne.

For ten years, Frankie Warren Pershing had been present in the general's thoughts even when she could not be at his side. Now she was gone, along with the couple's three daughters. With Frankie's death, the heart went out of Pershing. The man who had always looked younger than his years suddenly began to age. Pershing gave his son, Warren, over to two of his sisters, and the boy grew up at their home in Lincoln, Nebraska. Pershing then returned to spend a lonely winter in El Paso, separated from his family once again, but this time forever.

During the last half of 1915 and early 1916, violence along the Mexican–United States border increased considerably. The number of Mexican raids onto U.S. soil increased. In the Mexican province of Chihuahua, in January, 16 American mining engineers and officials were dragged off a train and executed by some of Pancho Villa's men, who shouted, "Death to the Gringos! Viva Villa!"[65] In early March, 500 followers of Villa—*Villistas*—raided and looted the tiny U.S. border town of Columbus, New Mexico—a village so remote it had no electricity—killing 17 Americans. Although President Wilson did not want direct military confrontation with the Mexican *pistoleros*, he could no longer stand by without acting.

American military forces would have to ride into Mexico and hunt down those responsible, including Villa himself. Pershing was chosen to lead the expedition into Mexico.

Pershing began to form a complete campaign force, including two brigades of cavalry and one of infantry, as well as artillery support. The day of pack mules was about to pass—Pershing purchased 30 trucks for the expedition. A unit of eight JN-3 biplanes, the First Aero Squadron, was also included. Among the cavalry units was Pershing's old command from the days of the Spanish-American War, the Buffalo Soldiers of the 10th cavalry.

On the morning of March 16, 1916, Pershing's troops were ready to move out and cross the border into Mexico. They had gathered at Columbus, and the entire town came out to cheer and see them off. Pershing was consumed with his command, trying to replace his sorrow over the loss of his family with duty. Despite having trucks, airplanes, and a few automobiles, Pershing still led his troops on horseback.

As Pershing brought his forces into the mountainous desert lands of northern Mexico, he had no delusions about the difficulties that lay before him. He had said privately that locating Villa would be like finding "a rat in a cornfield."[66] He hoped for a short campaign, knowing that a lengthy mission would require the cooperation of the Mexican government, and Carranza did not intend to provide such support for American intervention into his country.

Pershing's force looked like nothing in U.S. military history to that date. It was an army of transition, old elements mixed with new. Trucks mingled with horses and planes flew overhead above cavalry units. Pershing used the planes to drop parachuted dispatches to his far-flung cavalry units in the field. Historian Gene Smith provides a rich picture of how the expedition looked as it advanced south of the border:

> Pershing headed south through great plumes of dust raised by the hooves of horses from ground that had not seen a drop of rain in months, equipment thumping and thudding and squeaking, sabers and pistols and pennons [narrow banners] and the horse-drawn artillery pieces, the trucks and a few touring sedans groaning in the rear, laden as they were with forage for the horses and rations and ammunition for the men, great slabs of bacon strapped side by side with drums of gasoline, tins of hardtack, bedding, rifles, and bags of water for the steaming radiators. Men wore goggles and tied bandanas over their mouths.[67]

Mobility was Pershing's goal as he plunged his men deep into Mexican territory, covering 140 miles (225 kilometers) in less than two days. He dispatched flanking columns of fast-moving cavalry in search of any sign of Villa. The difficulties of moving such an extensive force became obvious immediately. Daytime temperatures reached 115°F (46°C), and the night air dropped to freezing. Sunburn cracked the skin, and the alkaline water caused blisters. Trucks became stuck, not in mud, but in ancient desert ruts. Rattlesnakes crawled into bedrolls. After less than two weeks in Mexico, snow fell in the high plateaus, freezing horses to death.

Yet Villa was nowhere in sight. Even after Pershing had marched his men hundreds of miles into Mexico, dispatched scouting missions over every mountain range in sight and beyond, and had his Curtis Jennys comb endless miles of terrain from the air, he had not found Villa. When a newspaper reporter asked the general where he thought Villa was, Pershing answered matter-of-factly:

"Your guess is as good as mine."[68] Although he tried to make the best of his difficulties and frustration, he slept little, and when he did so, it was on a bedroll out in the open. He did not even have a desk or camp chair. He ate the same food as his men. Pershing also took up smoking again, after a largely smokeless ten years.

Pershing's forces encountered an endless number of rural villages and broken down haciendas. Mexican troops appeared here and there, but they offered no assistance. Instead, they asked probing questions about Pershing's intentions in their country. They wanted to know how many men he commanded and how far he intended to take his expedition into Mexican territory.

After two weeks in the country, some fighting that involved Villa's forces occurred. That morning, units of the 10th cavalry, Pershing's old command, reached the Agua Caliente ranch, west of Bustillos Lake. There, the 10th cavalry encountered about 200 Villistas and a short gun battle opened, with the Americans routing the Mexicans. The Villistas took up positions in a gully after being pursued for several hours by cavalrymen. On the morning of April 2, the 10th attacked again, as pistol shots and machine gun fire ripped the desert air. The battle ended with a scattered retreat by the Villistas, who slipped into the hill country beyond the skirmish site.

By now, Pershing's men were 350 miles (563 kilometers) from the United States – Mexico border and their search for Villa had proven fruitless. The general had moved his headquarters 40 miles (64 kilometers) south of the Mexican National Railroad line. A story surfaced that Villa had been spotted just to the south, bound for the railroad town of Parral. As the Americans moved in pursuit, however, local Mexican authorities, including one of Carranza's generals, advised the advance units of cavalry to turn back and proceed no farther. When a

Pershing's search for the outlaw Pancho Villa drew the general deep into Mexico, where his troops were met with hostility from both townspeople and government forces. The prolonged campaign strained U.S.-Mexican relations and proved to be only an embarrassment to American forces. Villa was never captured.

unit of 100 cavalry reached Parral, they were greeted inhospitably by the local military general. Crowds in the town's streets shouted "Viva Villa!" as the Americans entered. Outside the town, a Carranzista force attacked the small number of cavalrymen, killing several. Pershing received word of the skirmish at Parral two days later, on April 14. The attack changed the general's mind about his mission. Now that Mexican government troops were firing on his troops, his strategy became defensive, rather than offensive.

Government officials in Washington, D.C., exchanged messages with officials in Mexico City after the Parral incident. The Carranza government made it clear that it wanted to talk seriously about "the withdrawal of [the United States] forces from our territory."[69] By the end of

April, the Carranza government had laid down guidelines defining any future role that American forces might play in Mexico. By May, the Carranza government was demanding the withdrawal of Pershing's expedition from Mexican soil altogether.

As the Carranza government began to take a hard line that spring, however, so Wilson and Pershing dug their heels in, too. Pershing considered using force to occupy all of northwestern Chihuahua permanently after he moved his headquarters hundreds of miles back to the north. The expedition and its goal were soon lost in an international face-off between the Mexican and American presidents. Relations between the two governments worsened after a heated fight broke out at Carrizal, 60 miles (97 kilometers) east of Pershing's headquarters, between Mexican government troops and the Americans in late June, resulting in dozens of U.S. casualties.

Diplomatic relations between the two countries were being strained to the limit. Carranza proposed "direct and friendly negotiations" between his country and the United States on July 4. Wilson accepted the offer. The U.S. president was no longer focused on events in Mexico, but had turned his attention instead to the conflict in Europe. On the high seas, German submarines were menacing American merchant ships and sinking unarmed passenger vessels, and American civilians were among the casualties. While intent on keeping the United States out of the war, Wilson daily monitored a distant fight that seemed to be drawing ever closer to home.

Meanwhile, Pershing's command in Mexico continued for another seven months. Although chasing Villistas continued in a haphazard manner, the American general understood that his campaign had been an overall failure, and each day his troops stayed in Mexico after the Parral and Carrizal skirmishes was an embarrassment for the

United States. Pershing received orders to discontinue his long-distance cavalry patrols. His men largely remained in the Chihuahua towns of El Valle and Colonia Dublan, where Pershing had established his first head-quarters in northern Mexico. Pancho Villa's main army was resurfacing, raiding Mexican towns and killing Carranzistas. Carranza's forces did little in response. Pershing's men did nothing.

Finally, in January 1917, Pershing received orders to return his expedition to the United States. By February 5, he and his columns of now highly experienced field forces crossed the Mexican-American border at Columbus, New Mexico, as military bands played "When Johnny Comes Marching Home."

7

"Lafayette, We Are Here"

Within two months of Pershing's return to Columbus, New Mexico, after almost a year tracking Pancho Villa, President Wilson went before a joint session of Congress, requesting a declaration of war against Germany. Since the opening days of the war, Germany had begun to engage in unrestricted submarine warfare against any ships the Germans deemed supportive of the Allied nations, which included France and Great Britain. Americans had died in those attacks. Then, in March 1917, President Wilson received a copy of a message sent by the German foreign secretary in Berlin to the German minister in Mexico City. The note suggested that secret negotiations be held between the Germans and the Carranza government. In

With the unsuccessful Mexican campaign over, President Woodrow Wilson turned his attention to the war in Europe. German submarines had long been attacking Allied ships, and now Germany was suspected of conspiring with Mexico against the United States. In 1917, Wilson brought America into the war.

return for Mexico's alliance with Germany in any future war involving the United States, the Germans agreed that their government would help Mexico recover the territory of the American Southwest, land the United States had acquired from Mexico in the Mexican War of the 1840s. The message, called the Zimmerman Note (or Telegram), infuriated Wilson and the American public.

On his return from Mexico, Pershing was made commander of the southern department of the army, stationed at Fort Sam Houston. A month after he took up his duties, however, Congress declared war on Germany, and any plans Pershing might have had for his immediate future were sidelined. One month after the war declaration, Pershing received a telegram from his father-in-law, Senator Warren, asking the general how well he could speak French. Puzzled, Pershing responded that he spoke the language well. A second telegram arrived a few days later, this one from Major General Hugh L. Scott. It said that Pershing might soon be tapped for command of any American forces sent to Europe.

Pershing took a train to Washington, D.C., to meet with General Scott, who informed him directly that he would be commanding a division of troops once they reached the shores of France. Two days later, Secretary of War Newton Baker changed Pershing's orders. Pershing was to leave for France immediately. By late May, Pershing had been secretly whisked aboard the ship *Baltic* for a voyage across the Atlantic. The ship's portholes were covered with paper and it traveled without lights so it would not be seen by lurking German submarines. The *Baltic* also traveled with an escort of several navy destroyers.

As the darkened *Baltic* cut through the icy Atlantic waters, Pershing had much to think about. He had been placed in command of an army that largely did not exist yet. The regular army had only 5,000 officers and a smaller number of reserve officers. The number of cannons in service that spring of 1917 was fewer than 600. In case of a full-scale war, the amount of ammunition in storage would last less than one day. American air power consisted of fewer than five dozen airplanes, and many of them were not fit for combat. The war into which Pershing was headed had already devastated Europe's people, resources, and morale. The fighting had become a stalemate with both sides—the French, British, and Italians against the Germans, Austrians, and Bulgarians, plus a host of lesser combatant nations—erecting elaborate trenchworks where soldiers burrowed into the ground for protection.

Now the Americans were coming. Pershing understood that he was being sent into a war that was more complicated, larger in scope, and had more at stake than any fought to that date in American history. Onboard the *Baltic*, the general and his staff worked on the details of creating, training, and equipping an American army of perhaps one million men.

Before Pershing arrived in France, he had studied the war and the various tactics and strategies on which both the German-led Central powers and the Western European Allied powers had relied since 1914. Even before visiting a single battlefield, he was certain of one thing: His troops, the young American men who were enlisting or would soon be drafted, would not fight to hold defensive trenches. The stalemate of trench warfare must be broken, he told his aides and fellow officers.

Pershing and his staff landed in Great Britain, where they were given a grand reception that included military bands, a meeting with the British monarch, King George V, and luncheons with the prime minister. After several days, Pershing was crossing the English Channel to France. A train ride brought him to Paris, where he was greeted warmly by throngs of French citizens. A French military band, the *Garde Republicaine*, played "The Star-Spangled Banner." Riding in an open touring car, Pershing was overcome:

> Perhaps nothing similar had ever occurred in Paris, certainly not in the life of anyone living. Flowers bought by shopgirls from their meager earnings, or by war workers, or soldiers' wives, simply poured from windows. Little American flags waved everywhere in people's hands. Windows blossomed with them. Children screamed from the trees they had climbed; and on the sidewalks their elders wept.[70]

When Pershing arrived in England, he was given a grand welcome by King George V. Pershing knew, however, that ahead lay the challenge of breaking the stalemated trench war in Europe. With few men and little equipment, Pershing would have to rely on his skills as a leader and strategist.

Excited French women broke past police barriers desperate to kiss Pershing's hands. From every corner of every street came shouts of "*Vive Pershaing!*"

The day after his arrival in Paris, Pershing was taken on a visit to the tomb of France's greatest military leader, Napoleon Bonaparte. As Pershing and his staff were guided down marble stairs, they saw glass cases containing personal military items that had been worn by the great French leader. An elderly French officer unlocked a case and removed a golden sword that had been worn by Napoleon at the Battle of Austerlitz more than an century earlier. He solemnly handed it to a surprised Pershing. It was the American leader's moment to demonstrate whether he really believed he was the answer to the Allies' problems in the war effort against the Germans.

As doubters looked on, the general did not miss the opportunity. He stepped forward with true military bearing, keeping his hands at his side, and bent forward to kiss the French military icon. The gesture immediately endeared him to countless French citizens.

Pershing also visited the tomb of another French military hero, the Marquis de Lafayette, who had served as an aide to George Washington during the American Revolution. Pershing laid a wreath at the site and was soon quoted as saying, "Lafayette, we are here!" The words were actually spoken by one of his officers, Colonel Charles F. Stanton. Pershing denied that the quote was his own for the rest of his life.

Because he had arrived before his troops, Pershing had time to plan his strategies and goals for the men he would command in Europe. He found the task before him a daunting one:

> The map does not tell it all. It's the situation *under the lines* of the map. The third year of the war! With Russia in, Italy in, Rumania in, and all the Allied armies in with their full man-power, they could not win. Look at what is expected of us and what we have to do and what we have to start with! No army ready, no ships to bring over an army if we had one. How [to] supply and transport an army across France after it is here?[71]

Despite his concerns about the fighting that lay ahead, Pershing was able to look at the military situation with an optimistic realism. "The German army is no superhuman army," he assured others. "It has been beaten before and can be beaten again."[72]

Allied commanders informed Pershing that they expected the American role to be nothing more than to serve "as a giant recruiting ground for the deplenished legions of His Majesty's forces and for the descendants of *La Grande Armee*."[73] The Allied army simply needed infantrymen. American officers were unnecessary, since commands would come from the British and French generals. The strategy would be theirs, and the Americans would just fill in the ranks of the armies of Great Britain and France that had been reduced by war. Pershing, however, had not been sent to this European war to do the other armies' bidding. "The United States will put its troops on the battlefront when it shall have formed an army worthy of the American people,"[74] said Pershing. He refused to take instruction from European generals who for three years had shown no more imagination on the battlefield than to order their men to emerge from their trenches and attack the enemy's lines, only to be slaughtered by machine-gun fire.

Within weeks of the general's arrival in France, the first of his men, the U.S. 1st infantry division, began to come to Europe as quickly as they could be trained at home and shipped out. American involvement in the fighting did not begin immediately, despite these first arrivals in June 1917. Americans did not reach the front lines of the fighting until late October. By then, many Allied commanders were beginning to believe that the American contribution to the war would be of little importance.

As American forces trickled across the Atlantic to join their comrades in Europe through the winter of 1917–1918, those under Pershing's immediate command found life difficult. They were outcasts of a sort. Other

Although Pershing was able to inspire the confidence of the French, the task of turning hastily trained American troops into an effective fighting force weighed heavily upon him. American troops did not enter the war until October 1917.

Allied soldiers looked down on them, since they were not yet participating in the fighting, even as reserve troops. During the first year that American forces were in Europe, they lost 200 men, a small number compared to the casualties suffered by the other Allies. Other problems plagued the Americans, too. They did not have enough food, shelter, guns, or clothing. Even their pay often came late. Despite these setbacks, by early 1918, the American army in France had grown to 250,000.

Then, just as many of the European Allied leaders began to believe they had Germany on the edge of surrender, having beaten them down with high casualties, the Germans launched a massive offensive on March 21, 1918. Along a 50-mile-wide (81-kilometer-wide) front, the Germans landed full force on British front lines, using every weapon at their disposal, including poison gas. When the British abandoned their field positions, the advancing Germans moved forward by 40 miles (64 kilometers), toward the French city of Amiens. They surprised the Allies so completely in late May at Château-Thierry that the Germans were able to march to within 40 miles (64 kilometers) of Paris. The French capital appeared to be on the brink of collapse. If the Germans continued to advance, the entire Allied line might be crushed and the war lost. Desperate for support, the French and British commanders requested reinforcements from the Americans. Pershing refused.

Pershing did not sit still entirely, however. He targeted the French town of Cantigny for an American assault. He ordered 4,000 Americans from the 1st division to recapture the town. Much was riding on how well Pershing's troops performed in the field at Cantigny. Failure might well mean having to abandon the idea of separate American field units, even before they had had a real chance to prove themselves. Pershing understood well what was at stake.

In the early morning hours of May 28, 1918, after a few hours of artillery bombardment on the town of Cantigny, Pershing ordered the 28th infantry regiment of the 1st division out of its trenches and toward the bombed-out town. The battlefield was littered with bloody corpses and burning bodies, and the stench of poison gas hung in the air. Despite firing a hail of enemy bullets, the Germans could not stand firm against this tide of fresh Allied troops. They began to fall back. Holding Cantigny, however, would not be as easy as taking it. German artillery rained down on the Americans, the fighting continued, and hundreds of Pershing's troops lost their lives. For three days, the Americans—"dirty, frightened, hungry, thirsty, sleepless for the noise"— held their ground against heavy German resistance. Their casualties were high, mounting to as many as one out of every three men. Still, they had won and held the field of battle, and Pershing was jubilant. "Dining with his staff, Pershing banged his fist on the table and shouted with joy."[75]

Into the Woods

It was to be the first of months of fighting for Pershing's men. On June 6, 1918, American forces met the Germans along the Marne River, as U.S. marines led the attack. The fighting was hellish, involving "[a]rtillery, gas, mortars, fire from flamethrowers, rifle bullets in sleets."[76] Much of the fighting centered in the Belleau Wood, where thousands of Pershing's troops fought against heavy resistance and counterattack. In his book, *The United States in World War I*, historian Don Lawson describes the battle in the Belleau Wood:

> Belleau Wood was not merely a well-defended German position.
> It was one solid wall of machine guns. The Marines moved

American troops met stiff resistance from German forces along France's Marne River. Facing gas, mortar, and a rain of gunfire, Pershing's young troops performed well and drove back the Germans. The fierce fighting, however, left only ruins in its wake.

forward without even the benefit of an artillery barrage before the opening attack. As they advanced against this rain of death, the Marines bent forward like men leaning against a hurricane wind. . . . For twenty-four hours a day during the next two weeks the Marines fought their way a savage yard at a time through this nightmare forest. Losses were enormous, yet no thought was given to retreat. On June 26 the following famous message was received by General Pershing: "Entire woods now occupied by United States Marines." And a few days later the French published an official order stating that Belleau Wood was to be renamed the Wood of the Marines.[77]

These were Pershing's men, young American men trained in a matter of months, steamed across the Atlantic in huge transport ships, and thrust onto a foreign battlefield in a war that many of them likely did not fully understand. Pershing was now commanding more than one million men in France alone, the largest American army under a single command in U.S. history up to that time. The 58-year-old soldier was proud of his men. As they struggled across French fields and farms with bullets and bayonets, Pershing fought for them, battling the European commanders who never gave up on their wish for American troops to fill their own ranks. Pershing and his men were putting new battles into America's history books: Cantigny, Château-Thierry, Belleau Wood, and the Second Battle of the Marne.

Fighting continued through the summer of 1918 as the Germans attacked Pershing's line, an assault he finally turned around in September. The battle involved more than 500,000 American forces. Here, as Pershing had always planned, the action took place out of the trenches, with much hand-to-hand combat—and tens of thousands of American casualties.

British and French commanders no longer asked about the capacity and resolve of American troops to fight. Pershing stayed in contact with his field commanders, driving them to victory. The American commander threatened subordinate officers with removal from their field command if they did not perform according to his orders or were tardy in taking action. This applied even to men he had known as friends for many years.

From September 26 through October 3, the Americans had the Germans on the defensive, pushing them back relentlessly. Then, on October 4, Pershing sent fresh troops, many of whom had already been in battle against the Germans, to face the best divisions Germany could deliver

Exhausted, wounded, and many suffering with the flu, Pershing's men fought an inch-by-inch battle with German forces in the forests of France. Pershing himself fought exhaustion but remained at his post, urging his men on. At last, the American forces broke through the Hindenburg line, forcing an armistice that would end the war.

to the front. A fiery Pershing was certain "we must maintain the battle until the enemy [is] worn out."[78] Death and disease stalked the American forces. By October 5, 16,000 of Pershing's men had the flu. Still, they fought on.

The fighting was tenacious and desperate on both sides, and the Germans only retreated out of "the forest a tree at a time and individual deeds of heroism were being performed hourly."[79] By mid-October, Pershing's army had advanced over territory formerly held by the enemy, consisting of an offensive line stretching out for more than 100 miles (161 kilometers) in length. This meant that Pershing commanded one-fourth of the entire Allied front. He often visited the front and spoke to his weary, shell-shocked forces: "Men, if you can stick this out a little longer I'll have you out of here in a few weeks." [80] The commander became physically tired, worn out by his responsibilities, but he kept going, just as he asked his men to do. Pershing refused even to take short naps at his own desk. He was determined to remain at his own post, no matter how he might feel or how exhausted he might be.

By early November, his advance units had broken the last point of German defense, the Hindenburg Line. Less than a week later, the German high command made overtures for an armistice. The following day, November 7, the German leader, Kaiser Wilhelm II, abdicated his throne and fled to exile in the Netherlands. On November 11, an armistice was signed at 11:00 A.M., ending the fighting of World War I. That evening, Pershing's jubilant staff held a party, dancing to records on a rickety Victrola. Even Pershing danced.

The Americans had tipped the scales of war in favor of the Allies, and in November 1918, everyone knew that. Pershing had seen his men to the battlefields of France and had led them and the Allies to ultimate victory. For 47 days, the tenacious American troops, backed by artillery, planes, tanks, and the stern leadership of General John J. Pershing, had fought against the best the German military could offer. Of that final battle, Pershing wrote:

> Between September 26th and November 11th, 22 American and 6 French divisions, with an approximate fighting strength of 500,000 men . . . had engaged and decisively beaten 43 different German divisions, with an estimated fighting strength of 470,000. Of the 22 American divisions, four had at different times during this period been in action on fronts other than our own. The enemy suffered an estimated loss of over 100,000 casualties in this battle and the First Army about 117,000. It captured 26,000 prisoners, 874 cannon, 3,000 machine guns and large quantities of material. [81]

A Private, a General, and Lots of Mud

In his various commands, Pershing was often extremely intimidating to his men. He believed it was important for a commander always to have a professional bearing, a cool detachment from his troops. This often frightened his men somewhat. One of his officers once put it succinctly: "He just scarified us."* On one occasion, however, a private did not let any feelings of fear stop him from carrying out his duty, even if it meant drawing Pershing's ire.

On a rainy night at his post, a 1st division private on guard duty along a road stopped a limousine. It was the staff car of General Pershing. One of the general's orderlies approached the private to inform him that Pershing was inside the vehicle and that he must pass through the checkpoint. The private told the orderly, Frank Lanckton, that he was required to have all occupants emerge from their vehicles to be recognized and identified before he could allow them to proceed.

The rain was beating down and the ground was a muddy morass at least a foot deep. The orderly returned to the car, and Pershing's aide, Colonel Carl Boyd, got out next, furious with the uncooperative private. His voice was angry as he told the young man, "Here, sentry, you better pass this car before you get into trouble." Again, the private was told that the general was inside. Once again, the sentry refused to let the car through, saying, "I don't give a damn. . . . Those are my orders."**

At that, Pershing slowly got out of the car and approached the sentry, his boots sinking in mud and "even the bottom of his overcoat picking up heavy streaks of soft clay."*** As he walked toward the guard, the sentry saluted and apologized for requiring his commander to get out of the car. Properly identified, Pershing returned to the limousine and moved on. Pershing ordered Colonel Boyd to get the name, rank, and serial number of the sentry. The next day, the general had the private promoted to sergeant. The bold private had acted properly, obeying his orders at all costs, and he was rewarded for it by General John Pershing.

* Quoted in Gene Smith, *Until the Last Trumpet Sounds: The Life and Times of John J. Pershing*, vol. 1. College Station: Texas A & M University Press, 1977, p. 164.

** Ibid., p. 165.

*** Ibid.

After the end of World War I, Pershing continued to serve until the mandatory retirement age of 64. In the end, however, he remained a soldier — and after his death at 87, he was buried beside his men at Arlington National Cemetery.

By the end of the battle, Pershing had commanded 1.2 million troops and had brought about the greatest military victory in American history to that date.

With the armistice in place, Pershing had accomplished much of his mission in Europe. He received congratulations from dozens of world leaders, including kings, ministers, and military figures, for his efforts in bringing about an Allied victory. The U.S. Congress honored him with a new rank: general of the armies. Some people thought Pershing should run for president, but he declined. "My country trained me as a soldier," he said. "I have had the fortune to lead its army to victory. That is enough." [82]

The commander immediately turned his attention to getting his troops back home to the United States. During the eight months following the armistice, Pershing remained in Europe, organizing the demobilization of his army. In March, his son, Warren, came over on an oceanliner and surprised his father, who had not seen him for two years. They traveled across Europe together, as Pershing met with world leaders, conferred with the British secretary of state for war, Winston Churchill, and dined with kings and queens. The general was honored at every stop, each city handing him special honors and granting him special citizenship. Oxford University even gave him an honorary degree.

By July 31, 1919, Pershing's command in Europe had been reduced to fewer than a dozen men, most of whom were his staff. It was time to go home. As he wrote in a letter to a friend, "My work is finished."[83]

Epilogue

Pershing boarded the oceanliner *Leviathan* on September 1, 1919, along with his son, Warren. Eight days later, they docked in New York Harbor, and on September 9, Pershing rode on horseback in a parade down Fifth Avenue, leading the men of the 1st division, the great veterans of the Great War.

Pershing would never see combat again. Upon his return to Washington, D.C., he took up his duties as general of the armies, a desk job for the most part. He spent the next five years restructuring the American army, ordering many commanders to attend war colleges. Pershing had seen the future of warfare in Europe, and he was determined to have the U.S. military fully prepared when war broke out again, as he was certain it would.

His life became more relaxed than it had been in years. There were dinners with dignitaries and close friends, a speech before Congress, parades, and gifts from admirers, everything from a horse given by an American Legion chapter in New York to a Cadillac sedan. He had become a great symbol of a new American military tradition, a war hero and a celebrity. He spoke before groups from state legislatures to local Kiwanis Clubs. When he took a train to northern Missouri and visited his old hometown of Laclede, the entire town turned out to see its favorite son. Old students from his days as a schoolteacher were there, and the general remembered their names. One said she would like to see him become president someday. He scolded her, "Mollie, don't get such foolish notions in your head."[84]

In 1924, Pershing turned 64, the mandatory retirement age for members of the U.S. army, and on September 12, he closed out a military career that had begun with his graduation from West Point in 1886. For the first time in nearly 40 years, the aging general, who had seen action in the Pacific, Asia, Cuba, the Great Plains, Mexico, and France, was a civilian. In an interview, he made clear what he had learned during his years in uniform. "There's no 'glory' in killing," he said. "There's no 'glory' in maiming men. There are the glorious dead, but they would be more glorious living. The most glorious thing is life. And we who are alive must cling to it, each of us helping."[85]

In retirement, he lived as fully as he could, traveling to Europe again and seeing old battlefields. He visited Warren, who was at private school in Switzerland. He was appointed head of the American Battle Monuments Commission. In this role, he selected the designs for war monuments, including the one erected in memory of the Belleau Wood battle.

Pershing also spent the next several years writing his

memoirs. In 1931, his book, *My Experiences in the World War*, was published. It earned him the Pulitzer Prize.

As the years passed, Pershing remained in Washington, D.C., and could be seen around the city, taking long walks in the parks. The government still called on him from time to time, such as in 1937, when President Franklin Roosevelt asked Pershing to go to the coronation of the new British monarch, King George VI. Although Pershing attended that event, he tried to refuse as many invitations as he could. In his later seventies, he was often sick and suffered from frequent colds that led him to spend winters in Arizona. That same year, Warren became engaged to be married the following spring. Two months before the wedding, Pershing fell seriously ill with heart and kidney problems. Many people believed he would die, and newspapers ran headlines about his rapidly sinking condition. Despite the grim predictions, Pershing recovered and managed to attend Warren's wedding on April 22.

Nearly 20 years had passed since the end of World War I, and another major conflict had erupted in Europe. As World War II began in 1939, the German army marched into France and occupied Paris. President Roosevelt asked Pershing to become the U.S. ambassador to the German-controlled Vichy government of France. Pershing turned down the offer. His days of public service were over. Nevertheless, when the United States entered World War II, military commanders came to Pershing yet again. He gave advice to U.S. Army Chief of Staff George Marshall, who had served under Pershing in France during World War I.

Pershing lived to see the Americans and their allies win World War II in 1945. His final years, however, were quiet, sad, and reclusive. He wrote fewer letters and saw fewer visitors. The public seemed to forget the great World War I commander. New heroes replaced him—President Harry

Truman, General Dwight D. Eisenhower, and George Marshall who became Truman's secretary of state.

Just two months short of his eighty-eighth birthday, Pershing died on July 15, 1948. Four days later, his coffin was delivered to Arlington Cemetery in a horse-drawn caisson. George Marshall attended, as did Generals Eisenhower and Omar Bradley. Veterans of World War I and a host of others came to pay their respects to the great general.

Before his death, Pershing had arranged to be buried at Arlington so he would be near the soldiers he had commanded across dozens of battlefields. Even in death, he chose to be a soldier, nothing more and nothing less.

CHAPTER 1

1. Quoted in Frank E. Vandiver, *Black Jack: The Life and Times of John J. Pershing*, vol. 1. College Station: Texas A&M University Press, 1977, p. 201.
2. Ibid., p. 202.
3. Quoted in Gene Smith, *Until the Last Trumpet Sounds: The Life of General of the Armies John J. Pershing*. New York: John Wiley & Sons, Inc., 1998, p. 52.
4. Ibid., p. 54.
5. Ibid.
6. Quoted in Vandiver, p. 203.
7. Ibid., p. 204.

CHAPTER 2

8. Quoted in Gene Smith, *Until the Last Trumpet Sounds: The Life of General of the Armies John J. Pershing*. New York: John Wiley & Sons, Inc., 1998, p. 4.
9. Quoted in Frank E. Vandiver, *Black Jack: The Life and Times of John J. Pershing*, vol. 1. College Station: Texas A&M University Press, 1977, p. 4.
10. Quoted in Smith, p. 6.
11. Quoted in Vandiver, p. 6.
12. Quoted in Smith, p. 11.
13. Quoted in Vandiver, p. 14.
15. Ibid., p. 21.
16. Quoted in Smith, p. 15.
17. Quoted in Vandiver, p. 23.
18. Quoted in Smith, p. 21.
19. Quoted in Frederick Palmer, *John J. Pershing: General of the Armies, A Biography*. Harrisburg, PA: The Military Service Publishing Company, 1948, p. 22.

CHAPTER 3

20. Quoted in Frank E. Vandiver, *Black Jack: The Life and Times of John J. Pershing*, vol. 1. College Station: Texas A&M University Press, 1977, p. 49.
21. Quoted in Gene Smith, *Until the Last Trumpet Sounds: The Life of General of the Armies John J. Pershing*. New York: John Wiley & Sons, Inc., 1998, p. 29.
22. Ibid., p. 30.
23. Ibid., p. 32.
24. Quoted in Frederick Palmer, *John J. Pershing: General of the Armies, A Biography*. Harrisburg, PA: The Military Service Publishing Company, 1948, p. 31.
25. Quoted in Vandiver, p. 119.
26. Quoted in Palmer, p. 33.
27. Quoted in Everett T. Tomlinson, *The Story of General Pershing*. New York: D. Appleton and Company, 1919, p. 60.

28. Quoted in Vandiver, p. 127.
29. Quoted in Smith, p. 46.
30. Ibid., p. 48.

CHAPTER 4

31. Quoted in Frank E. Vandiver, *Black Jack: The Life and Times of John J. Pershing*, vol. 1. College Station: Texas A&M University Press, 1977, p. 172.
32. Ibid.
33. Quoted in Gene Smith, *Until the Last Trumpet Sounds: The Life of General of the Armies John J. Pershing*. New York: John Wiley & Sons, Inc., 1998, p. 50.
34. Quoted in Vandiver, p. 191.
35. Ibid., p. 186.
36. Ibid., p. 206.
37. Quoted in Smith, p. 54.
38. Ibid.
39. Ibid., p. 55.
40. Quoted in Vandiver, p. 211.
41. Ibid.
42. Ibid.

CHAPTER 5

43. Quoted in Gene Smith, *Until the Last Trumpet Sounds: The Life of General of the Armies John J. Pershing*. New York: John Wiley & Sons, Inc., 1998, p. 57.
44. Ibid.
45. Ibid., p. 77.
46. Ibid.
47. Ibid.
48. Quoted in Richard O'Connor, *Black Jack Pershing*. Garden City, NY: Doubleday & Company, Inc., 1961, p. 78
49. Ibid., p. 82.
50. Ibid., p. 90.
51. Ibid., p. 91.
52. Quoted in Frank E. Vandiver, *Black Jack: The Life and Times of John J. Pershing*, Vol. I. College Station: Texas A&M University Press, 1977, p. 388.
53. Quoted in O'Connor, p. 87.
54. Quoted in Smith, p. 97.
55. Ibid., p. 100.
56. Ibid., p. 99.
57. Quoted in Vandiver, p. 439.
58. Quoted in Smith, p. 101.
59. Ibid., p. 102.
60. Quoted in Vandiver, p. 458.
61. Quoted in Smith, p. 105.
62. Ibid., pp. 105–106.
63. Quoted in Everett T. Tomlinson, *The Story of General Pershing*. New York: D. Appleton and Company, 1919, p. 102.
64. Quoted in Smith, p. 111.

CHAPTER 6

65. Quoted in Gene Smith, *Until the Last Trumpet Sounds: The Life of General of the Armies John J. Pershing*. New York: John Wiley & Sons, Inc., 1998, p. 122.

66. Ibid., p. 124.

67. Quoted in John S. D. Eisenhower, *Intervention! The United States and the Mexican Revolution, 1913–1917*. New York: W. W. Norton & Company, 1993, p. 215.

68. Ibid., p. 262.

69. Quoted in Smith, p. 142.

70. Ibid., p. 144.

71. Quoted in Eisenhower, p. 280.

CHAPTER 7

72. Quoted in Gene Smith, *Until the Last Trumpet Sounds: The Life of General of the Armies John J. Pershing*. New York: John Wiley & Sons, Inc., 1998, p. 154.

73. Quoted in Frederick Palmer, *John J. Pershing: General of the Armies, A Biography*. Harrisburg, PA: The Military Service Publishing Company, 1948, p. 97.

74. Ibid., p. 98.

75. Quoted in Smith, p. 157.

76. Ibid.

77. Ibid., p. 161.

CHAPTER 8

78. Quoted in Gene Smith, *Until the Last Trumpet Sounds: The Life of General of the Armies John J. Pershing*. New York: John Wiley & Sons, Inc., 1998, p. 184.

79. Quoted in Don Lawson, *The United States in World War I*. London: Abelard-Schuman, 1963, p. 78.

80. Quoted in David F. Trask, *The AEF and Coalition Warmaking, 1917–1918*. Lawrence: University Press of Kansas, 1993, p. 140.

81. Quoted in Lawson, p. 114.

82. Quoted in Smith, p. 197.

83. Quoted in John J. Pershing, *My Experiences in the First World War*, New York: De Capo Press, 1995, reprint of 1931 edition, pp. 388–389.

84. Quoted in Frederick Palmer, *John J. Pershing: General of the Armies, A Biography*. Harrisburg, PA: The Military Service Publishing Company, 1948, p. 348.

85. Quoted in Smith, p. 226.

EPILOGUE

86. Quoted in Gene Smith, *Until the Last Trumpet Sounds: The Life of General of the Armies John J. Pershing*. New York: John Wiley & Sons, Inc., 1998, p. 238.

87. Ibid., p. 257.

88. Ibid., p. 293.

1749	First generation of the Pershing family arrives in America.
1860	John Joseph Pershing is born on September 13, 1860, in Laclede, Missouri.
1876	Sixteen-year-old Pershing passes his examination for teaching certification and teaches as Laclede Negro School.
1880	Enrolls in the First District Normal School in Kirksville, Missouri.
1882–1886	Attends and graduates from the U.S. Military Academy at West Point.
1886–1890	Assigned to cavalry duty at various posts in New Mexico, including Fort Bayard, Fort Stanton, and Fort Wingate.
December 1890 –January 1891	Assigned to duty in South Dakota during the Ghost Dance campaign.
1891–1895	Teaches as professor of military science and tactics at the University of Nebraska, Lincoln; earns law degree from the university in 1893.
October 1895 –December 1896	Assigned to duty at Fort Assinniboine, Montana, where he serves as commander of the 10th cavalry, an African-American regiment.
December 1896 –May 1897	Assigned to duties at the headquarters of the army in Washington, D.C.
Summer 1897	Returns to duty at Fort Assinniboine for a few weeks.
June 1897 –May 1898	Serves as an instructor at West Point.
Summer 1898	Fights in the Spanish-American War with the 10th cavalry in Cuba; receives the Silver Star.
Fall 1898 –Summer 1899	Assigned to duties in Washington, D.C., including organizing the Insular Bureau, an office established to administer former Spanish territories.
Fall 1899 –1903	Takes up duties as adjutant general of the Filipino districts of Mindanao and Jolo; negotiates with Moro leaders and engages in the Battle of Bacleod.
1901	Promoted to captain in the regular army.
1903	Installed as a member of the General Staff Corps in Washington, D.C.
January 1905	Marries Helen Frances Warren of Cheyenne, Wyoming; immediately after their marriage, the Pershings sail for the Philippines.

1905	Serves as military attaché to Japan for nine months; during this tour, he observes the Russo-Japanese War first-hand.
September 1906	Frankie Pershing gives birth to the first of the Pershings' children, Helen Frances; Pershing is advanced in rank to brigadier general by President Theodore Roosevelt.
March 1908	Frankie gives birth to the Pershings' second child, Anne Orr; Pershing begins to have health problems; the family leaves the Philippines in June.
Summer 1908–November 1909	Pershing spends much of his time in treatment for illness and heart problems, including three months in a New York sanitarium and at the Army and Navy Hospital in Hot Springs, Arkansas.
June 1909	Pershings' third child, Francis Warren Pershing, is born.
November 1909–December 1913	Pershing family returns to the Philippines, where the general has been appointed governor of the province of Moro.
May 1912	Fourth Pershing child, Mary Margaret, is born.
Spring 1914	Pershing takes command of the Presidio in San Francisco, California.
April 1914	Pershing ordered to take two infantry regiments to Fort Bliss, outside El Paso, Texas, in response to perceived threat of Pancho Villa along the Mexican-American border.
August 1915	Frankie and the three Pershing girls die in a fire at the Pershing home at the Presidio; Warren survives.
March 1916–February 1917	Pershing leads U.S. forces on an expedition to capture Pancho Villa; Villa is never captured.
September 1916	Pershing is appointed a major general.
May 1917	Pershing sails to Europe as the newly appointed commander of the American Expeditionary Forces (AEF).
Summer–Fall 1918	Pershing leads American forces in significant battles against the German army; his victory in the Argonne Forest will help ensure the ultimate defeat of Germany.
September 1919	Returns to the United States to serve in Washington, D.C., as general of the armies.
1921	Appointed army chief of staff.
1924	At age 64, Pershing retires from the U.S. army.
July 15, 1948	Pershing dies at Walter Reed Hospital outside of Washington, D.C.

Braddy, Haldeen. *Pershing's Mission in Mexico*. El Paso, TX.: Western Press, 1965.

Bullard, Robert Lee. *American Soldiers Also Fought*. New York: Maurice A. Lewis, 1939.

Eisenhower, John S.D. *Yanks: The Epic Story of the American Army in World War I*. New York: The Free Press, 2001.

————. *Intervention! The United States and the Mexican Revolution, 1913–1917*. New York: W.W. Norton & Company, 1993.

Lawson, Don. *The United States in World War I: The Story of General John J. Pershing and the American Expeditionary Forces*. London: Abelard-Schuman, 1963.

Martinez, Oscar J. *Fragments of the Mexican Revolution*. Albuquerque: University of New Mexico Press, 1983.

O'Connor, Richard. *Black Jack Pershing*. Garden City, NY: Doubleday & Company, Inc., 1961.

Palmer, Frederick. *John J. Pershing: General of the Armies*. Harrisburg, PA: The Military Service Publishing Company, 1948.

Pershing, John J. *My Experiences in the First World War*. New York: Da Capo Press, 1995.

Smith, Gene. *Until the Last Trumpet Sounds: The Life of General of the Armies John J. Pershing*. New York: John Wiley & Sons, Inc., 1998.

Smythe, Donald. *Guerrilla Warrior: The Early Life of John J. Pershing*. New York: Charles Scribner's Sons, 1973.

————. *Pershing: General of the Armies*. Bloomington: Indiana University Press, 1986.

Tomkins, Frank. *Chasing Villa*. Harrisburg, PA: Military Service Publishing, 1934.

Tomlinson, Everett T. *The Story of General Pershing*. New York: D. Appleton and Company, 1919.

Trask, David F. *The AEF and Coalition Warmaking, 1917–1918*. Lawrence: University Press of Kansas, 1993.

Utley, Robert M. *The Last Days of the Sioux Nation*. New Haven, CT: Yale University Press, 1963.

Vandiver, Frank E. *Black Jack: The Life and Times of John J. Pershing*. College Station: Texas A&M University Press, 1977.

TIM McNEESE is an Associate Professor of History at York College in Nebraska. Professor McNeese earned an Associate of Arts degree from York College, a Bachelor of Arts degree in history and political science from Harding University, and a Master of Arts degree in history from Southwest Missouri State University. He is currently in his 27th year of teaching.

Professor McNeese's writing career has earned him a citation in the "Something About the Author" reference work. He is the author of more than fifty books and educational materials on everything from Egyptian pyramids to American Indians. He is married to Beverly McNeese who teaches English at York college.

CASPAR W. WEINBERGER was the fifteenth secretary of defense, serving under President Ronald Reagan from 1981 to 1987. Born in California in 1917, he fought in the Pacific during World War II then went on to pursue a law career. He became an active member of the California Republican Party and was named the party's chairman in 1962. Over the next decade, Weinberger held several federal government offices, including chairman of the Federal Trade Commission and secretary of health, education, and welfare. Ronald Reagan appointed him to be secretary of defense in 1981.

During his years at the Pentagon, Weinberger worked to protect the United States against the Soviet Union, which many people at the time perceived as the greatest threat to America. He became one of the most respected secretaries of defense in history and served longer than any previous secretary except for Robert McNamara (who served 1961–1968). Today, Weinberger is chairman of the influential *Forbes* magazine.

EARLE RICE JR. is a former design engineer and technical writer in the aerospace industry. After serving 9 years with the U.S. Marine Corps, he attended San Jose City College and Foothill College on the San Francisco Peninsula. He has devoted full time to his writing since 1993 and has written more than forty books for young adults. Earle is a member of the Society of Children's Book Writers and Illustrators and the League of World War I Aviation Historians and its sister organization in the United Kingdom, Cross & Cockade International. He belongs to the United States Naval Institute and the Air Force Association.